Journeying

Journeying East

Conversations on Aging and Dying

Victoria Jean Dimidjian

Parallax Press
BERKELEY, CALIFORNIA

Parallax Press
P.O. Box 7355
Berkeley, CA 94707
www.parallax.org

Parallax Press is the publishing division of Unified Buddhist Church, Inc.
© 2004 by Victoria Jean Dimidjian.

Photo Credits: Ram Dass © Lisa Law; Frank Ostaseski © Michael
Venera; Joan Halifax © Tom McCall; Thich Nhat Hanh © Nang Sao;
Michael Eigen © Steve Kahn; Rodney Smith © Elizabeth Vidgeon;
Sister Chan Khong © Jessica Tampas; John Wellwood © Ted Gabbay;
Norman Fischer © Robert Hoffman

Library of Congress Cataloging-in-Publication Data

Dimidjian, Victoria Jean.
  Journeying East : conversations on aging and dying /
  Victoria J. Dimidjian.
    p. cm.
  ISBN 1-888375-36-1 (pbk.)
  1. Aging—Religious aspects—Buddhism. 2. Dying—Religious
aspects—Buddhism. 3. Spiritual life--Buddhism. I. Title.

  BQ5435.D56 2004
  294.3'444—dc22

                          2004013307

Cover and interior design by Gopa & Ted 2, Inc.

Contents

Preface by
Christina M. Puchalski, M.D.   7

Introduction   9

Ram Dass   15

Frank Ostaseski   27

Joan Halifax   47

Thich Nhat Hanh   61

Michael Eigen   71

Rodney Smith   87

Sister Chân Không   103

John Welwood   115

Norman Fischer   131

Resources   151

To Vanessa Grace who will join our world in July 2004
And her parents, Karina Dimidjian and Edouard Lecomte

Preface

IN *Journeying East*, Victoria Dimidjian converses with men and women who have embraced the mystery of living and dying and share their experiences and their wisdom. This book provides important tools for all of us as we journey within to discover who we are deep within ourselves.

As a physician who cares for aging and dying people, I have been privileged to walk a very special journey with my patients. As people face their own mortality, questions arise about meaning, purpose, and value. What is my worth to my family and to the world? What value has my life had for me? Was my life worth it? Should I have done something different? Should I have been someone else? This book raises these questions and provides some surprising and healing responses.

My patients have taught me that illness, loss, and dying are opportunities for growth. Some of my patients call their illnesses blessings because the illness enables them to see themselves and life in a new light. Even in the midst of deep pain and suffering, they are able to find meaning and joy. They begin to see the life around them more intensely. Many of my patients talk of being fully in the moment, aware of all the richness around them. Every moment is a gift. They learn about their souls beyond their ego. As Ram Dass writes in *Journeying East*: "I have learned about suffering and love, about compassion and caring, through this aging, this time beyond the ego."

Increasingly, the healthcare system is recognizing that the spiritual dimension of our lives in an integral part of healing. Scientific data demonstrate that patients who find meaning and purpose in the midst of suffering have good quality of life even as they deal with chronic illness or with dying. It is critical that healthcare systems and society recognize this spiritual dimension in people's lives. But more importantly, we need to be willing to walk the journey toward our dying and face those issues in our lives and in our souls. This book is a welcome light to help us along the path.

Christina M. Puchalski, M.D.
Director, The George Washington Institute for Spirituality and Health
George Washington University

Introduction

Journeying East brings together conversations with nine men and women recognized around the globe as important teachers of Eastern and Western wisdom and understanding. Each generously offered their time to talk, taking hours to explore the themes of this book. Each has made unique contributions to humanity and is now living and learning about the later stages of life firsthand. Their conversations contain wit, wisdom, and words worth long periods of reflection and meditation. I found myself listening to each conversation time and time again, cherishing their energetic engagement with life's deepest questions. I hope you will find yourself reading and rereading these conversations too, learning from each dialogue and opening to new understanding and joy about life's journey.

Each person interviewed began his or her life journey by studying and training in a traditional discipline and then expanded it to integrate aspects of psychology, anthropology, social work, theology, creative arts, and many other streams of human creativity. Further, and perhaps most important, each person has integrated a broad and active definition of spiritual engagement in their work. For many of these teachers, their spiritual dimension has expanded and strengthened in mid/late-life. In *Jerusalem Moonlight*, poet, teacher, and Zen priest Norman Fischer journeys to Israel, where he experiences and articulates the human suffering he sees in both Palestinians and Israelis. And when his spiritual community in San Francisco was later in crisis, he tells of turning to Thich Nhat Hanh, a Vietnamese poet, Zen Master, and teacher, who guided him toward deeper understanding and conscious action. Each person interviewed here weaves knowing, doing, and caring dynamically together so that head, heart, and hands nurture life and support positive growth and change.

Supporting growth and change has been my own life's mission as a teacher, writer, parent, and activist. And now, nearing the end of my academic career, the opportunity to take a sabbatical to explore end-of-life issues with those whose works were respected worldwide seemed a perfect late-life journey. If I hadn't been in Washington, D.C. on the morning of September 11, 2001, when the plane crashed into the Pentagon, perhaps my just-begun sabbatical would have proceeded, as intellectuals are prone to do, with lots of reading, ruminating, and writing. But instead I got behind the wheel and drove for two days back to my little island home in southwest Florida. The next day, a hurricane hit, taking my home's roof and my last sense of security and control.

So my sabbatical began with immersion into all that seemed then overwhelming: aging, destruction, suffering, loss, and death. As I sat with waves lapping around the foundations of my stilt house, I looked back at my life. I'd been touched by loss and death early, and a recent relationship had broken, leaving shards still sharp under my feet. My divorce so long ago seemed easier than this latest loss. Sitting in silence, I was thrown back to memories of slowly losing my mother to melanoma two decades earlier and the terrible night my father's car crashed at four in the morning.

I was just four–and–a–half the night my father died. It took twenty-five more years before I learned his life story. Only then did relatives tell me of my parents' late-night argument, his driving away in anger heading back to his family in Chicago, a journey terminated in the dark rain. For years I had bad dreams during stormy nights. Not until I found his grave in the Michigan countryside did they subside. I knew then in my heart what my professional training told me, that healing comes from knowing, from finding the words to grieve and let go.

I'd built a life of teaching, writing, social activism, and spiritual growth. I had completed graduate work in child development and counseling, worked as a therapist, taught about families and children for three decades, and written books and articles about personal healing. I'd also built an academic career and lived with my family in remarkable places. But now I was aging and experienced being regularly overlooked, even denied as I entered later life. Walking on the beach that September of 2001, it seemed time to fully face aging and dying. So I read. I sat breathing deeply, being still. I turned the news off. Life felt filled with the reverberations of suffering and loss as I set off on the road to start the interviews in late October.

I went first to Santa Fe for the Upaya Center's ten-day retreat on death and dying with Joan Halifax and a team of practitioners skilled in caring for the dying. Then I went on to San Francisco to visit the Zen Hospice. I traveled from northwest Washington state to southwestern France. My job was to learn as the project unfolded, and learn I did! So many more resources on aging and dying are available in this new millennium than in the mid-seventies when I began teaching. Then our culture was just beginning to articulate end-of-life experience and to study the long-term effects of loss, death, and denial. Ernest Becker's *The Denial of Death* and Elisabeth Kubler-Ross's early work on dying opened pathways toward acceptance of suffering and loss.[1] In the three decades since, we have come much further in seeing life and death as deeply connected, even if most of us are still not able to accept them as one.

As I look back on the journey of these conversations and all I've been given during the process of journeying east, four themes stand out, linking the nine interviews.

First, *aging and dying are emerging as significant themes for my generation, those who came of age in the Sixties and changed consciousness in our culture.* In the Sixties, we were focused on transforming a military-obsessed society and ending an impossible-to-win war in Vietnam. Now, many of this same generation are focused on changing our culture's youth-oriented, death-denying traditions and affirming aging and late-life learning. The youngest interviewees were in their late fifties, the oldest almost eighty. Each articulated a new cultural model for living later years, aging, and embracing death. Seeing Ram Dass smile and hearing his words as he taught from the confines of the wheelchair brought new energy to my tired, well-traveled frame. When he spoke about wheeling himself through a recent peace march, his energy spread like expanding spokes across the group of us seated around him. For him, new frailty and vulnerability opened new doors toward peaceful acceptance of the interconnectedness of life and death.

Second, *the integration of Eastern and Western ideas continues to grow, strengthening each of us as we slowly construct a world for all life and all people.* Even after the nationwide shock of 9/11, the primary commitment of many of us to bringing the world together and addressing global tensions still seems to stand. My last interview was with Nobel Prize nominee Thich Nhat Hanh who said, "There is no journeying east, there is no journeying west. We live in the now." Would that our struggling world could manifest the wisdom of these words! But I do see a growing consciousness about interconnectedness each day, an increasing awareness that actions in one part of the globe reverberate everywhere.

This East-West integration is shown in research and teaching by people like John Welwood, who describes building a new psychological paradigm that dynamically integrates internal awareness, external connection, and spirituality. It is being done by people like Michael Eigen who works each day to expand and transcend the limitations of the psychoanalytic tradition. Others I interviewed have moved from research and service modes to establish spiritual communities where individual growth and spiritual change is supported. Rodney Smith in Seattle, Norman Fischer and Frank Ostaseski in the Bay Area, and Joan Halifax in Santa Fe work in this way on this side of the Atlantic while Thich Nhat Hanh and Sister Chân Không guide the communities that make up Plum Village in southern France and teach in countries across the globe.

Third, every interview deepened my understanding that *living and dying are one. How we live each day determines much of how we die.* John Welwood says, "So death is the ending of the body, and of the self in this particular form, but consciousness isn't anything solid, continuous, enduring. Experience is fresh at every moment. ... When we let go of our fixation on our thoughts, and let go of the baton that the last thought shoves into our hand, we experience a moment of both dying and coming alive at the same time."

And Frank Ostaseski, who has sat at the side of so many as they passed from life to death in the Zen Hospice, says simply, "You cannot go into the room where someone is dying and not pay attention. Everything is pulling you into the moment. And for me it is one of the most alive places to be, to be with someone who is dying. It's an extraordinary gift."

Fourth and finally, *our "knowing" is never enough.* Life is always larger than we can control or even at times comprehend. The life journey turns and twists, taking us where we need to go but sometimes not where we have planned. My two year journey took place in a world increasingly rife with tensions, new forms of terror, and war. Yet each leg of the journey brought new thoughts, unexpected and helpful adventures, and caring encounters. Challenges, especially those to my sense of personal control, created new moments for a deeper breath and greater focus on helping and giving. This has become even clearer as I accompany a family member into treatment after receiving a grave diagnosis some months ago, necessitating a re-evaluation of life plans and priorities.

These new turns in my life's journey bring me back to a deeper understanding that we are always learning to live each moment in new ever-more-real ways. Norman Fischer described how he spent a year writing a poem each day, placing that day of life on the printed page. He was motivated in part by the loss of four people close to him in a short period of time. Death was a teacher, he said, and added: "Dying is a way of living, a meditation practice, the most fundamental and most profound of all meditation practices. I think that death is our greatest teaching." He said it so simply, so clearly. Living and dying, being both alive and dead: that is the Zen challenge that inspires us each day. May this book bring you both support and inspiration.

ACKNOWLEDGMENTS

My first and deepest thanks goes to the nine men and women who generously opened their busy lives for interviews. I learned and gained more than I can say from each. Additionally, I would like to thank those at Parallax Press, especially editor Rachel Neumann and publisher Travis Masch. Initial support came from my university colleagues and former provost Brad Bartel, now President of Colorado's Fort Lewis College, who all supported my nontraditional journey. Many others at Florida Gulf Coast University also helped, especially my division staff Bridget Bloomster, librarian May Kay Hartung, and many students including Ali Lowe, Mary Herman and Shaney Kragh. My "Berkeley base" with Betty Pillsbury and Erika Wild nurtured my west coast work as did my sangha community here in Southwest Florida. Finally my family and friends who read, listened, and cared during these two years also deserve my heartfelt thanks, especially my Seattle triad: Sona, Chuck and Serena Dimidjian-Langdon.

1 Ernest Becker *The Denial of Death* (New York: Free Press, 1973)

Ram Dass
Speaking to the Soul

"Aging is a chance for a second childhood. We can go where we want to now—one can go from information to imagination to silence. And silence is so wise, so very wise. Going in, going in deep, going in silence, we go from being the do-er to being the be-er. That's aging."

"Living in the moment is like eating baklava—nutty on one plane, honey on another, and then on yet another plane it's flaky and falling apart."

RAM DASS is one of the forefathers in integrating East and West spirituality. His groundbreaking book, *Be Here Now*, (New York, NY: Three River Press, 1971) which explored different realms of consciousness, was published in 1971 and has sold millions of copies around the world. His books, tapes, speeches, and teaching have inspired those in the West who wanted to integrate Eastern understanding in new and dynamic ways. Ram Dass has long worked with the dying, with prisoners, and with the aging. In all venues, his ever-present humor enriches his deep spiritual understanding.

Ram Dass suffered a massive stroke in 1997 and has made a slow but progressive recovery, now doing some teaching and writing. I first met with him in a January 2003 workshop, the day after a 200,000-plus person peace march in San Francisco. Ram Dass shared with me his joy at seeing the outpouring of people as he wheeled his chair up the streets alongside parents with baby carriages, and waves of teens, adults, and the elderly. Witnessing his dedication and love as he interacted with the workshop on that warm Sunday afternoon, I understood better the "fierce grace" the stroke has blessed him with and was able to let go of fears I'd carried about the loss of my own life.

◖

Victoria Jean Dimidjian: Ram Dass, you have been a leading figure in linking Eastern and Western spiritual traditions for more than four decades. You've brought aging and dying into our Western social consciousness, and you've been a guide and inspiration in the hospice movement. I wonder if we could begin by going back to your early years, exploring what turned you towards the East and first brought death into your life.

Ram Dass: I was not spiritual, not growing up nor in the first part of my adult life. Back then I was very much the social scientist. Science was my religion.

It was at Harvard in the Sixties that Tim Leary brought me the magic mushrooms. I had always discounted religion as artificial. After the mushrooms, I was aware for the first time of the spiritual part of my being. We had a project going then, studying psychedelics at Harvard. One of our members was Aldous Huxley. I had taken LSD one Saturday night, and then the next Tuesday Aldous brought us *The Tibetan Book of the Dead*. In this book was the exact description of the experience I had with LSD. I learned that in the East there were maps of consciousness, levels of consciousness that our psychology had ignored. My whole understanding was transformed. All my friends—Allen Ginsberg, Tim Leary, Ralph Metzner—were beginning this journey too. We all had been changed, forever changed.

VJD: And begun a new life journey?

RD: Yes. Totally new. A friend of mine had a Land Rover and we explored India together.

He was an ex-Malibu surfer, and I hooked up with him in Katmandu. We took a walking trip across India from Buddhist temple to Buddhist temple. I liked Buddhism because it was so neat and clean! [Ram Dass chuckles, remembering that time.]

The ex-surfer wanted to visit his guru up in the Himalayas. Now I hadn't even known this guy had a guru; I thought he was a Buddhist! So I was responsible for this expensive Land Rover, going from the middle of India to the Himalayas with a guy who wanted to see a Hindu guru. I was not happy with that.

About fifty miles from where the guru was staying, we stopped for the night at the house of a friend. During the night I went out to use the outhouse, and I looked up at the stars. They were very intense. Very immanent. I felt the presence of my mother, who had died six months previously. Then I went on to the outhouse.

The next morning we drove the last fifty miles. We stopped at a little temple by the side of the road. My friend said, "I'm going to see my guru." And I said, "I'm going to stay here."

I was the guardian of the Land Rover! I wasn't interested in gurus. But finally my curiosity got the better of me. So I got out, crossed the road and climbed the hill. There were a few people standing and sitting around and in the middle was this old man. He was sitting on a wooden bed and wearing a blanket that kept falling off of him. My friend was on his stomach flat on the ground, his hands outstretched touching the guru's feet. And I am thinking as I watch, I'm not going to do that! I was so very Western then!

The guru said something in Hindi. One of the group translated to me, "Maharaji said you came in a big car. Maharaji said would you give the car to him." My friend who was still lying with his hands on his guru's feet said, "Of course, Maharaji, you can have anything you want." I started sputtering, "You can't! No! Not David's car!" And everybody was laughing. They were all laughing at me.

The guru motioned me over to sit down. Then he said, "You were out under the stars last night." I thought sure, plenty of people were out under the stars last night. That was probable. I said, "Yeah."

And then he said, "You were thinking about your mother."

I'd never thought such a thing was possible. My next thought was, uh-oh! If he can read my mind, then he knows all these things. I went through the catalog of things I wouldn't tell other people about me. The things I didn't want anyone to know. I'd always felt that anybody who knew me—

the real me, the one inside that nobody saw—anybody who knew that me would not love me. I'd been looking down at the ground while I was thinking all that, and I raised my eyes to meet his. And…he was looking into me with unconditional love.

It was…it was that my heart had never been touched.

VJD: So it was a moment of transformation?

RD: Yes. [He sighs deeply and takes a long pause] The change in that moment was that now I was not the ego. Now I was a soul. He mirrored my soul to me.

It's hard to know what words to use.

He opened in me a new place but also a new place in the universe. A new place from which to perceive reality. Now I was perceiving the whole, seeing the world from a viewpoint I hadn't known. I stayed with him six months then.

VJD: And your friend and the Land Rover too?

RD: That's right! Well, we didn't really need it anymore, did we?

When people come into our lives, even if unexpected, it gives us a new direction. So I stayed and studied, traveled to study with others, went back to the West. But I returned two years later with a number of other Westerners.

VJD: Can you say a bit more about the memory of your mother's death?

RD: Well…she was my first lover. She was the first contributor to my soul for this incarnation.

VJD: So her death must have taken you to the deepest place of loss…

RD: Well…probably not…not from what I know now. But I did hold her loss for a long, long time. I've lost so many, many people.

But there is more to that story. The next day the guru told me the organ that had killed my mother, the thing she had died of, and he said it in English! It was all in Hindi, except the word "spleen" was in English. It was pretty strange; that word jarred me into realization. Till then it had only been a romanticized connection.

"Your mother is a very high soul," the guru said to me. I asked, "Don't you mean *was?*"

Because she had died, you see. He said, "No, she is a high soul." In that instant I had a new relationship with my mother. Now we were both souls. Until then we had been only mother and son.

VJD: In limited bodies—

RD: Yes. In this incarnation, yes.

VJD: Are there words you can use now to describe without distorting the experience?

RD: I had an experience which engaged my heart. Totally and completely engaged my heart. A new way to live began then and there.

A doctor friend of mine came to see Maharaji. I remember the doctor said to me, "I'm not astounded that Maharaji loves everybody. He is a holy man. He is supposed to love everybody. But what astounds me is that when I sit in front of him, I love everybody." That was the power of his unconditional love.

VJD: It's deeply moving to hear this, especially in these dark days of stress and looming war—

RD: We can choose whether or not to get embroiled in all that negative stuff. But if our consciousnesses keep witnessing, then we will stay strong and intense inside. And there will be love inside. And we will transmit that from our own hearts to others' hearts, giving love and faith and care and so on.

Our work depends on us keeping strong so compassion comes out alive and strong.

VJD: You have recovered from the challenges your own body has given you after the stroke. Have you come to new realizations about aging and dying?

RD: I visualize us humans as beings with three conscious planes.

Consciousness One is the ego. That is the first one, the one we know best, the way we humans mostly live. Consciousness Two is the plane of the soul, the astral body. That's what I came to know in India, and what I live in now. And Consciousness Three, well, three is just three! [He laughs as he hears himself say this.] It also has all sorts of other names. But we humans fight over the names, don't we? So I just call it Number Three. It's the mystical part of each of us. Your Number Three and my Number Three are not just like one another, they are the same thing. We're made of the same thing but we have the other planes of being and, oh dear...the words, these words...

VJD: These things are very hard to capture in words. I remember in *Still Here: Embracing Aging, Changing and Dying*, you wrote of those three levels.

RD: Awareness, God, whatever you call Number Three, is beyond words and time. This is the Ground of Being. The soul yearns to return to that clear light. Ripening into God is the soul's journey.

VJD: And the mystics give us glimpses of it, but always say the words hide the experience.

RD: Oh yes, yes... Finding the right words is always hard. Now they come slower too...

VJD: Some of my students tell me they think it is so sad, this negativity about ego-identity. But to me it feels freeing. As if now is the time to let go of the ego.

RD: The ego is made up of mind, mind and thoughts. And thoughts are just things. It's a thing filled up with things. People who have materialist philosophies that turn on hearing, seeing, feeling, holding memories, they only know that ego. They have always to be feeding that ego. Filling it up.

VJD: Do you see aging as a time of growing?

RD: Here's what I think. In the earlier parts of your life, up through your mid-years, you switch identity from ego to soul by doing spiritual practices. In aging, life itself takes over a bit more. It becomes the practice that takes you to the soul. Aging is the stage of transition and change. The change that occurs is from being the ego, which has so many motives, to the soul, which has only one motive. The soul's one goal is to meld with the beloved, the One. That's what we as souls see as life's meaning. We look out at our lives as souls and we say, "How much has this life helped me approach the One?"

Or "How has my incarnation helped me become my soul?" I have learned about suffering and love, about compassion and caring, through this aging, this time beyond ego.

VJD: This seems connected to what happened in India, when the guru gazed directly into your core—seeing through the ego to the soul.

RD: Oh yes, because if that happens, it changes you. After that you just start seeing souls. I go to the supermarket and I see souls now. I don't see people in their roles, I see them as souls living out their karma.

VJD: Does this become easier as everyday desires seem less important?

RD: Aging helps, yes. No guarantees—but as desires are less important, it helps you see the identity with the soul.

My father is an example. I took care of him when he was very old. And our relationship changed, going from the rocky one of Jewish middle-class father-son to one where we were souls, just souls together. When we were both much younger, my Dad had constructed a three-hole golf course of which he was very proud. We were sitting on deck chairs looking out over the golf course at a sunset, a magnificent sunset. I said to him, "Beautiful, isn't it?" And he said, "Yeah, the grass is cut just perfectly."

Then near the end of his life when he was ninety, I sat next to him again, looking out on the sunset. This time we were holding hands. And he said, "Beautiful sunset, isn't it?" I said, "Sure is, it sure is a beautiful sunset."

VJD: It wasn't till the very end that he could be open to that?

RD: Well…I think he prepared for that time very beautifully. He took a wife after my mother died. I gave her away at their wedding. That relationship opened him, and it made the three of us great partners. She was a very spiritual person, and that kept Dad's life spiritual. He deepened his spiritual direction during those years with her, and with me too.

VJD: What was her dying like for you?

RD: Phyllis was deeply spiritual. But a real New England lady, argumentative, tough, willful, too. My job wasn't to tell her how to die but just to be with her.

She fought against death for a long time. She was strong, but the pain of the cancer was intense. It wore her will away. Four or five days before she died, she gave up the fight. Then we were together, just together. At the end she asked me to hold her up. I did. She took three deep breaths, long, slow, really deep. Then she died. That's how Tibetan lamas die, they take three long deep breaths and let go.

VJD: I'm struck by how different that was when compared to your mother's death.

RD: Well, my mother died in 1966. We've come so far since then. I've come so far. Just speaking with her about death, nobody was doing that. Everybody went into her room and told her she would be fine, then they went outside and said she'd be dead in two weeks. I held her hand and talked with her about it. It started me on the path to work with the dying.

VJD: Our parents and our elders can be such guides. It's wonderful but rare to have moments like the sunset you had with your father and the time with your stepmother. Are there ways to facilitate that?

RD: We facilitate it when we can be our soul. Just that. It's as simple as that. Then we can look into the soul of another, and that facilitates their spiritual practice.

VJD: So we come again to the theme of the work inside and the work outside in a flow, an incessant give-and-take.

RD: Right. In the same way that Krishna instructs Arjuna in the *Bhagavad-Gita*, saying, "Do what you do, but don't forget me." It means that you live your life on those two planes of consciousness. To be there, fully there, on both planes.

Oh my, now I've got another story to share. I remember my guru told me once that I should be like Gandhi. So I got those little glasses, you know, like he wore, but you know, those little glasses just didn't do it! But as I thought and I meditated about it, I remembered Gandhi's words, "My life is my message." That's one of those daily messages we have for being fully in touch with all our planes of consciousness.

VJD: In terms of your own daily life these days, Ram Dass, do you draw on other sources of strength you can share?

RD: Oh, I draw upon my guru. I look at the world the way he looked at the world.

VJD: You remain close?

RD: Oh yes, oh yes. I probably hook up with him most through my imagination. I call him my imaginary playmate. People say, "Oh, that's your imagination." You know how people talk! And then I say, joyfully, "Oh yes, that is my imagination!"

Aging is a chance for a second childhood. We can go where we want to now—one can go from information to imagination to silence. And silence is so wise, so very wise. Going in, going in deep, going in silence, we go from being the do-er to being the be-er. That's aging.

VJD: What about the hardship and pain that many of us feel is associated with aging?

RD: Pain is a potent attention-getter. I've learned what a delicate game it is to work with pain. It has to be fully experienced by the ego to be effective learning for the soul, but plunging in too deep locks you into the pain. You have to be on two planes at once, entering the pain fully yet being on the soul level at the same time. That's fierce!

Right after my stroke I asked, "Why this?" I had learned so much before, but now this. And then I found that is the lesson, the learning about fierce grace. Because the stroke brought me into my soul level, I call it grace. But it's not the easy grace I'd known from the past. The stroke took me right to the edge between its ferocity and Maharaji's love.

It's like learning to love Shiva or Kali, those deities that represent ferocity and destruction. It's learning to love whatever it is that brings me closer to God.

VJD: So aging demands that of you?

RD: Right. No putting anything in the way, not any more.

The pictures we need, the words we try to find. All just ways to be in the moment. That's what I am writing about now, that's what I want to open up. That's my hope.

Living in the moment is like eating baklava—nutty on one plane, honey on another, and then on yet another plane it's flaky and falling apart.

VJD: And all the honey just flowing out—

RD: And all these planes are there in this one moment—all different, all part of the moment!

VJD: Thank you for the gifts you've given me in this talk. When I walk my beach at sunset next I'll think of you, your father, baklava.

RD: And be there, be right there as the sun sinks down into that water. Without thoughts, just be there.

Frank Ostaseski
Living and Dying Each Day

"I work on myself so I can be of service to others; my service work with others is also for me."

"You cannot go into the room where someone is dying and not pay attention. Everything is pulling you into the moment. And for me it is one of the most alive places to be. It's an extraordinary gift."

"Being with the dying opens us to our own essential nature—very quickly and often very directly."

THE ZEN HOSPICE PROJECT, the first Buddhist hospice in the United States, first opened its doors in 1987. It is still the largest Buddhist hospice center in the country. Frank Ostaseski is the founding director of the Zen Hospice Project. He guided the organization until 2000, when he stepped down to lead the End-of-Life Counselor Training Program, an innovative program for students who wish to become better educators, advocates, and guides for the dying.

The Zen Hospice Project is housed in a Victorian building just a few doors down from the San Francisco Zen Center. I had last visited Zen Hospice in the first year of Frank's new project, when no one knew whether it would succeed. Now Frank and his staff have helped the first students graduate and are busy creating the team of medical, psychological, and spiritual teachers who will be part of the next year's program. Frank greeted me with a warm smile and pulled away from his work so we could sit in the front parlor and talk.

∽

Victoria Jean Dimidjian: Frank, you were instrumental in building a model of service and spiritual care for the dying at a time when death was still a taboo topic. Now bookstores carry shelves of materials on the end of life, and people buy videos on conscious dying. Is this a cultural change?

Frank Ostaseski: Yes, a whole cultural shift has taken place. Death has a place now, much more an honored place in our culture. Living and dying are connected. We are gathering what we know about that connection, pulling it together and working on it so we can advocate for change. But the challenge now is to ask if we are doing something fresh, something alive in ways of connecting the living and the dying.

VJD: And the End-of-Life Training Program is doing that?

FO: It is part of the process. Our faculty each bring unique perspectives. Ram Dass and Rachel Naomi Remen and Norman Fischer, many more, they all bring decades of experience with the dying. They've lived this change, and they're still exploring the spiritual dimensions of dying as they teach and serve the dying. And age themselves.

VJD: Like you, like me.

FO: Exactly. Our generation has demanded change at each stage of this living process. The end of life will be no different. What we're doing here now is gathering together what we have learned. We're reading the Buddhist sutras, learning from our service, and advocating for change. That's our work. It's fresh, I think, and so interesting, so full of meaning.

VJD: How did you come to this work? What path has your own life followed?

FO: Suffering first. It was a lot of suffering that led me into service. That's the easiest way to say it.

VJD: Tell me more that. Did it begin with your childhood?

FO: I grew up on the East Coast, about as far from here as you can get. My dad was a chauffeur on a big estate on Long Island. It was a very beautiful, somewhat protected environment. Idyllic really. And though we didn't have any money, we got to live in this very beautiful place. That was a tremendous benefit for me, that environment where I grew up. But my parents both died when I was young.

I first lost my mother when I was barely a teenager, and then my father just a few years later. I had three brothers. We were close in age but we couldn't help each other. In fact, we ended up scattered around the country. It was really traumatic. There was a lot of suffering before that time, lots of difficulties in my family, but losing them both marked me deeply. I know that eventually that drew me to work with the dying, but long before that I came to Buddhist practice and to service.

I was in a lot of pain. I came into Buddhism for the first time in New York when I was in my early twenties. At that same time I was doing service, working with kids from different cultures and then later with disabled kids. The service was really in part to avoid my own suffering. That's not so uncommon for people drawn to service. And it works for a while. But at some juncture we have to stop, turn inside, and really face our own suffering.

VJD: Traditional schooling didn't address this?

FO: Not at all! I'd gone through twelve years of parochial school on Long Island. It made me very distrustful of authorities, those people with all the answers. And I was coming of age just as the Sixties exploded. And I wasn't a traditional student with a stable family base; I couldn't connect with that life. I was on my own so early. Oh, I sat in classes at the community college and at Hofstra, where I went afterwards, but the learning I needed to do was with others in need.

This is what I thought until I was finally able to open to my own needs and the pain I was carrying. My first Buddhist exposure to a real teacher was in India. That was so long ago, back in the late Sixties. He was quite a master, a really charismatic figure. And then I traveled, I studied at various places across Asia. But when I came back to the States I really began to study. Because of the suffering in my family I became very suspicious of any kind of spiritual community. And I was particularly reactive to authorities, especially if they were any kind of father figure.

VJD: Was this in part the result of a parochial school education?

FO: Yes, twelve years of Catholic schools. I got a very good education, but I also got a good dose of hypocrisy. So I was reactive, like many people coming out of that experience. And I kept my distance from teachers. I was never in that kind of practice where I gave myself to my teacher. Even to this day I'm that way, to be honest with you. However, I have given myself to the practice. And the practice was the teacher for me. Different people have embodied that for me at different times, so I've been fortunate to have exposure to lots of good teachers.

Two parts of my life came together when I was about twenty-five. My early interest in Buddhism and Eastern thought and my service work fused, two streams running together. Soon after that I left the States for Central America, working with refugees there who were fleeing into Mexico, really running for their lives, for the next couple years. I saw people in such difficulty. I saw a lot of death.

My son was quite young then and I was just finding my way. I was a man searching, finding how to be a father. When I came back to the States, the AIDS epidemic was in full bloom. So that was another big influence on me eventually doing this work. I had many, many friends who were dying. I worked as an attendant for a while then. I took the midnight to eight AM shift, I really wanted to be at the bedside. It was always that time when things changed. In the middle of the night and early morning seemed to be when the suffering stopped. At the same time I was helping Jack Kornfield get the Spirit Rock Center started. Some friends told me about Zen Center wanting to get a hospice started, and that's when I came into contact with the beginnings of the Zen Hospice Project. The Center had always cared for their members who were dying, but now they thought they should extend this care to the community here in the city. Especially those most in need, AIDS patients and the homeless. And that's when I came to be fully involved here, back in 1987 as we were opening the doors. Lots of people were involved then, Martha de Barros, so many more.

VJD: Did you have guides to help you?

FO: Lots! Lots of important work was going on then. Elisabeth Kubler-Ross and Stephen Levine most of all. Elisabeth was first for all of us then. But Stephen was really important to me. Partly because, frankly, he stood a little outside the system. He was a kind of rebel. I liked that, I identified with him. And I imitated him even. That's what students do, isn't it? They imitate their teachers for a while until they find their own voice. I liked his blend of cross-traditions and his very extraordinary intuition. And he had a tremendous heart, unbelievable compassion. Watching those things in him helped evoke those in me. So I am totally grateful to him.

Another really important teacher was Jack Kornfield. He's a good friend now. One of the things I learned from Jack was his capacity as a synthesizer. I used to think that the only creative thought was original thought. However, Jack helped me to understand synthesizing in order to create something new. This has really influenced the way I do trainings and the teaching that I do. Of course many years of sitting on the cushion helped too!

VJD: What was it like to become the project's first director?

FO: The Zen Hospice Project gave me the opportunity to bring together mindfulness practice and service practice. I'd done hospice work, of course, and was deeply involved in mindfulness, but this melded them and made them one. It was a whole new way to do hospice work. You know, Rabindranath Tagore has a wonderful short story where he says that the paths through villages in India were always curved and winding. And then at some juncture children got sandals or shoes. And then the paths became very straight. I would say that I walked barefoot for a very long part of my life. Meandering around things, searching as I served. It wasn't until 1987, when the hospice opened, that I got my shoes on and started forward. Only when my hospice service and the mindfulness practice were equal parts of what I did, then I had two shoes leading me forward.

Most of the people who first came to live at the hospice had nothing. They were living on the streets. By most standards they had terrible lives, but each one brought a treasure. That was what was really fascinating. Finding out what happens when you bring together Marlee, the upper-middle-class woman who lives in Tiburon, with Jesus, the guy who's been living in the Tenderloin Hotel in the toughest district in San Francisco. You put them in the same room together and they find a common path. That's really interesting! Or Albee, a man who was immersed in his Buddhist practice, getting him to relinquish his practice and actually accept the guy Jesus just as he is, despite his distressing disguise.

VJD: Did finding those connections come easily for the caregivers or did you have to develop strategies for opening doors?

FO: When we first started Zen Hospice, I was overzealous. My vision was that this was the best Buddhist practice anyone could do. And everyone could do it. People would work in the kitchen and work in the garden and work in the hospice and sit on the cushions, everybody would do it all and we'd just rotate through. However, I eventually realized that caring for the dying isn't like any other job. It's really different. One needs a certain emotional stability and a very special kind of strength, even a social stability, to do this work really well.

Many who came to us here came because we were a spiritual center. They came from their own needs. They came to fall apart. This isn't a problem. It's appropriate, exactly what they need to do. But it makes caring for another's needs really difficult. We encountered two extremes: people who leaned too far into their own spiritual practices and started imposing them on others or those with a straight out "fix-it" mentality. The first ones might say, "Oh, it's really about just being there" or "Oh, I've just come to read to the dying" or "my meditation practice has helped with my knee pain, that's what I want to teach them." The first ones wanted to impart their spiritual practice while the others wanted to do direct action and make the suffering less somehow. The second ones wanted to do it right away. And what we did instead was helping people explore their own relationship to these issues, doing that deeply, intensely, rather than just developing skills.

We weren't so much interested in teaching skills as in helping people transform their lives and their relationship with death. Then they could be much more available to the dying. Only then. So we built our trainings around a retreat model which included periods of meditation practice but also continually exploring what our relationship was to what was arising.

That way of learning and teaching was what characterized Zen Hospice. We recognized from the get-go that hospice work is characterized by mutual benefit. I work on myself so I can be of service to others; my service work with others is also for me. This reciprocal arrangement helped us to avoid some of the pitfalls of what I call "helper's disease."

Maybe what I'm talking about is more like "helper's prison": the notion that here I am, the good guy, riding in on my white horse, and they're the poor, unfortunate dying one. Usually those of us who have done a lot of caregiving are so busy trying to prop up our identity, without clarifying our intention of why we go into caregiving in the first place. As I did. I really needed those people to suffer a lot so I could avoid my own suffering.

VJD: Does avoidance work? Does that hurting sixteen-year-old inside you ever go away?

FO: I find that I haven't really rid myself of a whole lot of neuroses. We're just better friends now. So by all means my younger child, my traumatized child, my angry sixteen year old, you know, they're all there. I'm a little more comfortable keeping them company now. And they also inform the way I work.

VJD: So you can have a dialogue with these other parts of you?

FO: Yes. And as I can include more dimensions of myself, I can reach into someone else. I know what it is like to be totally lost and helpless, totally without hope. I've had that. I know what it's like to be depressed, to feel you have no power left in your life. And so these parts of me, they aren't enemies to be avoided any more. But they continue to surprise me. They come up in ways I couldn't imagine. The doubt that was there as a sixteen-year-old still rises in me as a fifty-something year old!

VJD: How do you stay with this work? You've stayed with this domain for twenty years now.

FO: I'll say this...I don't think working with the dying is more important than any other kind of work. No more than working in the garden or taking care of our children. However—for me, just for me—I need something that really gets my attention because I'm sort of dull. Something that galvanizes me. Structured meditation practice helps me do that and to go into the room where someone is dying does that too.

You cannot go into the room where someone is dying and not pay attention. Everything is pulling you into the moment. And for me it is one of the most alive places to be. It's an extraordinary gift. Any place that I am holding starts to show itself. So I have to understand that when I am working with someone who is dying, I am also working on my own grief, my own fear, and my own inhibitions. When we are sitting on the cushion, the primary practice is mindfulness. This is extraordinarily powerful. But at the bedside two other elements enter. The first is unconditional presence. There's something that happens in the dynamic of this relationship between two people, one dying and one caring for the dying person, that deepens the exploration. And then another central factor when I am being a companion to someone who is dying is a deepening of inquiry, a door opening through the self.

Being with the dying opens us to our own essential nature—very quickly and often very directly. Meditation is a very slow path while this process can be very quick. And things can happen that would take years in therapy or meditation practice. The conditions are so conducive for this opening process, both for the person who is in the bed and the one beside the bed. The conditions are very intense, very unique, and very conducive to opening up because all of the ways we have identified ourselves—as a Buddhist teacher, a father, whatever it is—all of these are either stripped away by the dying process or they are given away, just discarded. This process is happening for the person who is dying but also for the caregiver. It's the very nature of the dying process that it melts the boundaries that have existed, sun and shadow, time and space, you and me. These boundaries are being literally shredded by the dying process. And these are the same conditions that exist in meditation except for the unconditional presence of the other and the door of inquiry swinging wide open.

Does this make any sense at all?

VJD: Oh yes, enormous sense. Have you thought about your own dying?

FO: Of course I reflect on this periodically. And pictures do come to me.

But I don't know how I will be with it or what it will be like. I don't want to be too Buddhist about this, but I really don't know. So what I am trying to do in my life is to be more comfortable with ambiguity so that regardless of how dying comes, it will be okay. Maybe it comes as a sudden death, maybe it comes when I'm comatose. I have no control over it.

Sometimes when I am in the line waiting on the grocery clerk and I'm impatient, if that was the moment I died, I wouldn't be so conscious. I hate to think that would be the moment that conditions my rebirth. But at the same time there are other moments—I was flying on the plane just the other day, and suddenly it dropped a couple thousand feet. Oooff! And the first thing that came to mind was may I be safe from all danger, may I be happy and peaceful. These things came right to mind because that was a habit I'd been cultivating. So I'm not so interested in this final moment of death being some ultimate experience but rather how I use the knowledge of death to inspire me to shift my habits now. I'm much more interested in that than I am in some dying peak. I know that some traditions in Buddhism believe this is the ultimate moment. But I don't have that sense. I believe the momentum of our habits is so strong—at least that's what I've seen—and that they carry into our dying regardless of the setting, the situation. So it's significant what habits we have created.

I've been with a number of Buddhist practitioners as they die. A good friend of mine, a thirty-year practitioner of Buddhism, died recently. What came up for him? His fundamentalist Christian upbringing that he had escaped at age six. There it was. And it was really powerful despite the many years of Buddhist practice. So we had to do some work together where he could make peace with this, face an inside full of fear and damnation. Unless we uproot those things now and bring them into the light of day now, we haven't a hope of doing it when we are dying.

VJD: How do you train people in this at the hospice? Is it systematic or do you just deal with issues as they arise?

FO: It's both! There is, of course, a structure and system to the training, but also it has to be adaptable to meet what is arising in the room. It has to be both. And more. In the first hours together we meet and talk about what brought us here. Not why did we come but what really brought us here. What single event? And then we start to invite death into the room.

Maybe it's a series of photographs. We ask each person to look at them directly, to see and taste and smell and touch, to find what attracts them and what causes them to hold back. That's a really simple exercise, and it's important to see both what attracts and what repels. Sometimes it's the same thing.

Once we have invited death into the room, we speak about impermanence, a central Buddhist teaching. That almost always leads people to a place of fear. And we encourage people to hang out in it. We don't give them a bunch of tools that they can use as a crutch or a wall. And that almost always brings people to a place of grief. And in that exploration of grief, people begin to literally touch their own suffering but also to be present for others. And once that presence is established, then we start to introduce skills. *Then* they can start to use skillful means, once they have become fully present in the moment.

VJD: It sounds like a dramatic contrast to traditional teaching. Is it that you begin with the heart, the living domain of life experience, and only after that is opened and engaged does the mind begin to work?

FO: I hope that we work with the mind too, not just the heart, but the mind, heart, and body. We do that in the volunteer training, working with each of these centers we've woken up. You know, if we were in the East, the door is often intense concentration, the focused mind. If you sit in a forest monastery in Thailand, that's the path. But in the West I think the gate is more often through the emotional life. It's a more accessible gate for most people. Death is a place people can get very overwhelmed. So we balance learning with really steady mindfulness practice and a sense of community. The bonds that get created in the groups are very important. We practice physical techniques as well—massage and walking meditation—but the emotional life is like the fast-rushing underground stream, and we need to keep dipping back into it.

What we had experienced in isolation before now becomes our common ground. A volunteer in our training once said that her parents had been Holocaust survivors and as a result she learned to grieve alone. She said, "I always kept my grief close to my chest. I was always ashamed. But here my grief joins me to others." There is a tremendous amount of freedom for people to include all their experiences, to go to deep places and recognize them as meeting places for working with the residents here. And so whether you're feeling anger or grief or fear or joy really doesn't matter so much as the connection. The question is, "Can you use it, can it be a context for coming together, for sharing the living moment?"

VJD: How have you put what you have learned at Zen Hospice into a form that is transferable to other people doing this work? How do you share what you've learned there?

FO: In trying to condense all the work we do here at Zen Hospice, everything just fell into five categories, what I now call the five precepts, each one deep and continually investigated by every caregiver so that we have to live our way into them. We can't just take them as rules, something to be done. We have to find our way into them every day.

The First Precept is: *Welcome everything and push nothing away.* The best way to explain what this means is through a story. We had a client in a psychiatric unit who had tried to take his own life. He felt there was no quality left in his life. I went into the unit and sat down in the chair next to his bed. I just sat quietly for a long time. Finally after this long period of silence, he said, "Who are you?" I told him. He said, "No one has ever sat with me this long before." I told him I get a lot of practice in sitting still. And then I said to him, "What do you want?" He said, "Spaghetti." So I told him we had good spaghetti at our house and why didn't he come live with us. He said OK.

So the next day he arrived at the hospice and when he came in we had a big bowl of spaghetti waiting there for him. And he ate it up, just smiling, not saying anything. Shortly before he died he said, "Frank, I want to thank you. I'm happier now than I have ever been." I asked him about when he wanted to kill himself, when he couldn't write in his diary and walk in the park or anything, when he didn't want to live any more. And he said, "Oh that. That was just chasing desire." I thought that was an amazing comment. This was a man who lived in a small hotel downtown. I said, "You mean that these activities aren't important any more?" "No," he replied. "It's not the activities that bring me joy. It's the attention to the activities. And now my pleasure comes from the coolness of the breeze and the softness of the sheets."

I don't know if this qualifies as conscious dying or not, but I thought it was extraordinary. We never taught him to meditate. He wasn't really interested in that. We just became a force of inquiry with him, and we created an environment in which whatever needed to happen could happen. It's the same environment we create when we sit on the cushion, the very same environment. When someone is sick and we lend them the strength of our bodies to get to the commode, we can also lend them the strength of our soul. We give them the calmness of our experience and engender the openness, the trust in the process.

Behind his suicide attempt had been absolute fear. Dying was his ticket out. He couldn't do it alone. He had a strategy to avoid the suffering. And instead we began to say, "We'll be with you in this. We'll look at this together." I mean, we didn't use those words. We just did it. And he understood it. Welcome everything, push away nothing, that's the first one.

The Second Precept is: *Bring your whole self to the experience.* We always think about bringing our skillfulness to the experience, but we also have to bring our whole self, including our weakness, our helplessness, and our fear. All of that heals too. Working with the dying is really intimate work, and we can't do it from a distance. We have to be part of the equation. I run in the opposite direction from most medical and academic training. I say let your heart get broken. Open your heart to this person. It's good that it breaks your heart. It's OK, hearts heal. They're soft muscles.

Yes, it is important to have some boundaries in our lives. We have to know how to do that. But at some junction we have to let the boundaries melt in order to really understand what this person's suffering is like.

The Third Precept is: *Don't wait.* Waiting is full of expectations. Too often we miss this moment waiting for the next one, waiting for the right one. Waiting for the moment of dying to arrive we can miss everything in between. When you asked earlier about what I want my death to be like, I know. I want my whole life to have been lived fully up till that moment. That's really what I want. So don't wait. When there's someone you love, tell them you love them. We had a board member who came to me when he was told his mother was dying. The doctor said she had six weeks to live. He came over and we visited. And he said he didn't know what to do.

He said, "Should I go back and be with her? She lives all the way in Toronto and here I am in San Francisco."

I said, "Just tell me about what is happening with you."

And he told me. And I said, "I think you should go tonight." And he did. He was sitting with his mother the next day when she died. Don't wait. Don't ever wait.

The Fourth Precept is: *Find a place of rest in the middle of things.* We can find our rest by bringing our full attention to whatever we're doing. We often think a rest comes from withdrawing our attention, but I find the opposite to be true. When I am fully engaged, I feel quite at rest.

Whatever activity is happening, if we bring ourselves completely to it, then there is nothing residual, nothing remaining afterwards. Suzuki Roshi used to be famous for eating his apples to a very, very thin core. That was the way he dealt with his life. He really consumed it. It's the Buddhist notion of sitting like your hair is on fire, with a sense of urgency.

If we are caregivers, when we're washing our hands, we just wash our hands. We give our attention fully and completely to that. When we're with the patient, we're fully with them, even if it's only for a short period of time. Here's an example. I work with nurses a lot, and some of them say, "Oh, I don't have time for all this stuff!" And then I say, "Well, when you are taking the patient's pulse, you're supposed to take it for a minute, right?" Lots of time nurses cheat, you know, taking it for thirty seconds, maybe even just fifteen seconds and then just multiply. So I suggest they take the entire thirty seconds—maybe a whole minute even, just steal it back from the HMO!—and give their full attention to listening to the pulse on this person's hand. That's an extraordinarily intimate act if you look the patient in the eye, not out the window. That's a way of bringing full attention to the moment, a way that refreshes us rather than depletes us.

There is a story that goes with this precept. There was an older woman, her name was Adele and she was very cranky, an eighty-six-year-old Russian Jewish lady. The night that she was dying they called me, and I came over to the house. I came in the room upstairs where she was sitting on the edge of the bed, bent a bit and breathing really erratically, "Huh-huh-huh!" She was actively dying then. And I sat on the couch, just close to her. There was an attendant with her, a really good worker.

She turned to Adele and said to her, "Adele, you don't have to be frightened."

And Adele lifted her head, saying, "Hey, honey, if this was happening to you, you'd be frightened!" Just like that, you know!

I stayed in the corner of the couch. A little later the attendant said, "Adele, you look like you might be cold. Would you like a blanket?"

Adele said in this big voice, "Of course I'm cold, I'm almost dead!"

I mean, she was a really tough lady. And I thought two things sitting there about what was really going on here. First, Adele wants straight talk about what's going on. She doesn't want slogans. She doesn't want to process her dying. She doesn't want to talk about tunnels of light or bardo states, nothing like that! She wants honest communication. Someone who can be with her in an authentic way. And second, there was fear. Despite all the interventions—she had pain medications, morphine, oxygen, all the things she needed—despite all that she was suffering. And it was manifesting in her breath.

So I always go towards suffering. So I got up, went to her, got very close and said, "Adele, would you like to suffer a little less?"

And she said, "Yesss."

And I said, "OK. I noticed when you are breathing, just at the end of the exhalation there is a little gap. I wonder what it would be like if you could put your attention there." I told her I'd do it with her.

Now this is an old Jewish lady. She doesn't care beans about Buddhism, meditation, none of it. She's shunned this stuff in the past. But right now she's highly motivated to be free of suffering. That's what gets most of us to sit on the cushion. If we know our own suffering, know what got us to sit on the cushion, we can use that as a meeting place for the suffering of someone else.

So she said OK. And then we were breathing together. I gave her a little bit of guidance but very little. I was encouraging her to rest in that pause. And as she did that you could see the fear in her face just draining away. Really amazing. And then she died. She had found her place of rest. Nothing changed, you see, all the conditions were the same. She was still dying. But she'd found a place of rest, right there in her breath. As caregivers we have to keep that principle right there, finding a place of rest in the midst of everything.

The last precept, the Fifth Precept, is: *Cultivate the don't know mind.* This means meet every moment in a fresh way. There's a corollary teaching by Dogen that says "not knowing is nearest."[2] And not knowing is most intimate. We have to stay very close to something to know it, like how we would walk through a cave at night, sticking close to the walls and the ground. Being with the dying is like that. We have to relinquish our preconceived ideas. I don't mean we need to throw out our tools or our expertise. I've got a really good toolbox but I'm not going to place it between me and the client.

VJD: So you don't impose your knowing on another person?

FO: Right! So we can walk with them in this process, continually inquiring about where we might be, not standing back and talking a particular view. This practice can help us be aware when the mind contracts or the body contracts. This capacity to not know, to be willing to be that intimate in the connection, that we're not driving it but accompanying it. This is the core of the training we do at Zen Hospice. These are the five precepts we use here and I find they have usefulness in other dimensions too.

VJD: Where do you see all this going? What changes in this work do you see ahead?

FO: Our generation has always wanted choice. In everything, in every way. If you go to Starbucks, you can get ten different kinds of lattes. I bought a stereo yesterday. I looked it up on the Internet and there were just too many different choices. It was impossible. I went to the store, and they had two receivers, and I asked, "Which one should I take?" We talked, I took one. We love choice, even when it makes us crazy! And so I'm sure this generation, as we keep getting older, will demand choices about dying. We are going to demand a menu of choices when we die: who is around us, how we die, where our bed is, and what help we get for starters. Health care, as it is currently set up, is not really ready for this.

VJD: Are you referring mostly to mainstream health care?

FO: I mean all the health care systems, mainstream and complementary health care. Both of them have certain rigid views and the belief that their way is *the* way. I remember sitting at California Institute for Integral Studies years ago as they were developing a program in holistic health care. They'd invited a number of people to this daylong gathering to talk about it. I watched as people introduced themselves first thing, and each one described their practice as "holistic" and yet by that description eliminated other practices represented around the table.

Our generation is going to want to pick and choose from mainstream and complementary medicine. And all the existing systems—including hospice care, which also tends to have rather rigidly defined criteria and methods—all the systems will be challenged to adapt and change. And as that happens, I also think people are going to want a single individual to be a guide, to assist and help with the choices at the end of life. Our End-of-Life Counselor Training is unique in preparing such guides. It prepares a single person who can be an educator, advocate, and guide. It is someone who can help sort through the maze of social and health care services, the myriad of choices that must be made. They can help you not only think about *where* dying takes place—home or a hospital or somewhere else entirely—but also advocate for the soul in the dying process. They are trained to be guides who can help plan for the unfolding process.

These counselors aren't like an advance scout to blaze the trail. I liken them much more to midwives who help a woman to discover her own way, direct her back to her own resourcefulness. The midwife uses the stuff of that woman's life to help her give birth. She knows the baby is going to come out, no question about that, but just telling the woman that doesn't reassure her. Her role is much more active than that.

VJD: So their goal is to really be with the person during the process?

FO: Exactly! There is an enormous need for this kind of an individual during the dying stage of life as our culture is confronted with so many thousands who are going to be dying thoughtfully, consciously, actively. New, very creative forms of caring are going to be born. And I have no idea what those are! I can speculate on some of them, but I'm not so interested in that at the moment. What I am interested in is creating a network of individuals ready to respond to this cultural change. This is a network of innovative, creative, adaptable, flexible people who will serve as educators and change agents in the communities or institutions.

VJD: So new ways of working will emerge?

FO: Yes, the ways will emerge just as they did in the birthing movement. But, you know, the other place we can look to about this is what happened in the AIDS epidemic. The AIDS epidemic seems like ancient history for some people, but those of us who cut our teeth in service during the Eighties know that something was created out of nothing. The systems we now take for granted—support groups, advocacy, individuals becoming self-aware about their medical conditions and choices—these things didn't exist before.

Recently we've seen the women's breast cancer movement adapt lots of those tactics and demand change, too. If I look at the twentieth century and identify the great spiritual movements, I'd choose two: Alcoholics Anonymous and what was stimulated by the AIDS epidemic. And even though I have troubles with part of what AA stands for, I'd say it's widespread effect on the culture was important and huge. Our culture's response to AIDS has been enormous too and much faster-paced. Huge sections of our population have had to rethink issues about sexuality and dying and have had to push for change real fast. Of course I feel it more being in San Francisco, but this has been all across the country.

The hospice community had to grow by leaps and bounds too in response to AIDS. Even though the AIDS community sometimes rejected the hospice movement. Nonetheless, people started talking about death, facing it in a big way. Not since World War II have we done that. Because death was now coming home, and people had to talk about it. And because the subject of death entered family discussion, the community, the home, the workplace discussions, people began to ask the next set of obvious questions. If death is inevitable, then how do we want to lead our lives more fully? That's truly the exciting part about putting death into the equation; not how do we prepare for the moment of death, but how do we lead our lives knowing that death will come to us?

VJD: Given the movements you've just identified, how do you see Buddhism as part of this culture?

FO: Wasn't it Arnold Toynbee [the English historian and philosopher] who said that the greatest event of the twentieth century was Buddhism coming to the West? I'd agree that it is right up there. But Buddhism has been changed by two important factors in the West. The first is feminism. Women's place in our culture has fundamentally changed the way Buddhism is practiced in the West.

The second encounter, which is happening right now, is Buddhism's encounter with service. Buddhism has matured in the West, and what was once understood to be a rather self-involved kind of practice is now stepping more fully into other facets of life. In traditional Zen practice, we sit facing the wall. I think things like the Zen Hospice Project are turning the practitioner away from the wall and into service to the world. I still feel that wall right behind me, supporting me. I wouldn't abandon that practice. But the forms of Buddhism that emphasize interconnectedness are growing in popularity. I think the encounter with service will be a tremendous shift.

In large part the West has been rooted in the Judeo-Christian framework which holds a tenet of charitable acts, a beautiful tradition. But charity hasn't changed anything. Charity emphasizes difference, the "I" and the "Other." What Buddhism can bring to this is the melting of Self and Other. The action of service is not about either me or you. In the action of service we join something bigger then either of us, the service of the Whole. We're already seeing it now. All the more mature Dharma communities have some kind of service practice going on. This was rare fifteen or twenty years ago but now it's growing across the country and the Western world. This is a new dialogue that I'd like to encourage.

VJD: All the turmoil after September 11 and the latest fury about a possible war with Iraq, all that has made these months dark, worrisome for many of us. Yet you seem so optimistic.

FO: I see signs of change everywhere. I'm only recognizing what is happening now. I'm not creating it. I haven't always been that way, but I feel very hopeful today. I have for the past few years now. I've always had a rather critical view of life, growing up as I did, doing the service work in so many places of struggle and pain. But I feel pretty optimistic now, even with the terrible tragedies in our world.

I don't know if Buddhism will find its way into our culture the way Christianity did. But the effects it is having—particularly the place of mindfulness practice—are filtering into all dimensions of our society. Just look at Jon Kabat-Zinn's stress reduction classes. They are in more than 2,000 hospitals across the country. Now if he had called it "Buddhist Meditation 101" no one would have bought it! But now we have HMOs across the country that are paying for people to go to stress reduction classes.

In terms of the future, I think that American Buddhism has the stream of meditation practice merging with the practice of service and that will change it fundamentally. American Buddhism is trying to find its own voice and its own shape. It won't be a recreation of what is in Japan or Thailand or Tibet. The well is deep and rich, and we should draw upon it. But what American Buddhism become will be new and will look different than anywhere else. Who knows what it will be in another twenty-five or thirty years? But as this happens I will be a voice advocating for us to examine our relationship to service. I think it will deepen Buddhist practice and it will deepen service. There has yet to be a new form combining them dynamically, but I think it is being created right now.

2 Dogen is a thirteenth-century Buddhist teacher who brought Soto Zen to Japan.

Joan Halifax
Embracing the Unknown

"Working with the dying, you are constantly reminded of what matters: love, kindness, generosity, and our interconnectedness."

"Life by life, death by death, how we live and die is being transformed."

JOAN HALIFAX has immersed herself in teaching and learning about dying for three decades. She is a spiritual leader in her community in New Mexico and around the globe, a social and peace activist and organizer, and a guide across wilderness expanses and mountain ranges around the world. Halifax has traveled, studied, and collaborated with Alan Lomax, Stanislav Grof, and Joseph Campbell. In 1979, she founded the Ojai Foundation in California, a living laboratory for the dynamic combination of Eastern and Western approaches to human growing and social change. Joan left Ojai at the end of the eighties and founded the Upaya Zen Center in Santa Fe the next year. She was ordained that same year. Soon after founding the Center, she started the Upaya Prison Project, which offers programs in meditation to prisoners across the state of New Mexico. Roshi Joan has consistently used her life experience as the platform for learning, teaching and practice. Her life's story has been thematic in each of her seven books as well as the 6-part tape series Being with Dying (Sounds True Audio). Her teacher Thich Nhat Hanh has said of Halifax: "The truth of suffering contains the truth of emancipation...This understanding is at the core of Joan's work and life."

I talked with Roshi Joan at Upaya Zen Center in Santa Fe. We met in the morning after an amazing workshop in which she and Tempa Dukte

Lama had spent a day exploring and teaching Buddhist and Bon death and dying practices. This was the first time such teachings had been offered to Westerners. Her honesty in recounting the story of the highs, lows, struggles, and achievements over her six decades sparkled like the sun glinting on the glaciers at 20,000 feet.

∽

Victoria Jean Dimidjian: Roshi Joan, you have been one of the most open Buddhist teachers on a personal level. How did you come to this open boundaries way when you are a part of a tradition of such hierarchy and definitions?

Joan Halifax: In Asia biography is not so important, you know, and the personal is not of such relevance, really, no true meaning. But in America our stories are where we begin. Biography, psychology, stories of our lives, that is where we start in the West.

And I'm a woman. I live in connection. I learn, I grow through connection. So all of that makes it easier to open, to let the story be part of the teaching. I think the hard part is that the boundary between me and anything is small, the veil is very thin. So it's not always easy for me in terms of my life being such a public and transparent experience. There are times I would just like privacy, a quiet life. But I've accepted this way that has come to be who I am. I've put myself in this situation, living with this transparency, and I am very comfortable with it. My Dharma name is "Chan Tiep." In Vietnamese it means "true continuation." The flow of life continues over, around, under the walls, beyond the boundaries.

VJD: Some teachers have grown into the style of teaching from the self, but it seems from your earliest writings you were open in that way. From the beginning you saw yourself as not only a teacher but as…

JH: A student to life.

VJD: To life?

JH: Yes! Everything is a teaching for me. I have to look at my whole life. I have to connect the inside and outside because I have a lot of responsibility, not just for myself but for lots of other people. I have to learn from every part of my experience. Constantly. It's not just theoretical, it's a continuous process of self-analysis, the practical experience of doing that inside as I work with others.

VJD: Is this process something you learned along the way or was that always who you were?

JH: I think that it's part of my personality. I had a lot of illness and suffering as a child. I had a lot of experiences with death that made me question and search inside. I realized the only way I could know others was to know myself. I think my own experience of suffering is inspiring for a lot of people. They can relate to the truth that I have been through such elemental destruction and have always come back up whole.

VJD: You said in your first book, *Fruitful Darkness*, that you were intuitively unwilling to go down into the self while in your twenties. Yet you did. You seemed to write then of fear but also of an absolute determination to explore what lay deep inside.

JH: Absolutely! Unwillingness comes from fear and fear causes sickness, resistance, anxiety. But I wanted a whole life, a whole continuous life.

For that to exist, I have to be constantly open to the inner and outer life at all time. I have to be vigilant. That's essential to my survival and my capacity to be of service to others. So I don't have a very lazy attitude or a lot of patience, especially with things that hold people back. I don't accept the walls some live with all the time.

VJD: Yet you seem committed to helping other get through their barriers...

JH: Yes. It's the only way to go forward. Relationships are the context where we receive the encouragement to go deeper and delve into more of what we really are. I learned from my father, my sister, my mother, the African-American maid who became the closest person to me when I was young and sick, all these relationships helped me to start this life journey.

They were all essential at that start.

Later, I had a science teacher who was on the boat at Pearl Harbor and got his face blown apart. Mr. Fitzgibbons. I'm sure he is long-gone now but he taught me, helped me.

Later still it was Alan Lomax who was my inspiration, mentor, and good friend. I worked for him for years, traveled with him and learned, learned so much. People like Stan Grof, my ex-husband, and Joseph Campbell and Huston Smith—they all lived this intense self-exploration. My Buddhist teachers also benefited me. Each brought me further…

It's interesting that there have been no women in this way, not in adulthood! Yet my closest relationships have been with women, the earliest ones with my mother, my sister, the African-American woman who raised me. And then my Dharma sisters, women who have lived profound lives and gone through fires themselves. These women have been essential, they are still essential.

So as I look at my life now in my sixtieth year, I recognize that men have had a very important role in inspiring and guiding and teaching me. But the relationships that have been more subtle and enduring, if not more important, have been the relationships with women. First in my family and then the women Dharma teachers who have dared to step out and assume some kind of responsibility for their lives and their work for the benefit of others. And it is primarily with women that I share this work of teaching compassionate care of the dying.

VJD: Your Buddhist teaching and care for the dying has been a new realm for us in the West. How did Buddhism begin for you?

JH: Well, I was a person of the Sixties! I cared about human rights, so the civil rights movement was a natural channel for me as was the antiwar movement. But even though it was all about social change, it involved a lot of adversarial dynamics. During that time I started reading Buddhism, first Krishnamurti, then D.T. Suzuki and Alan Watts. And I heard about Thich Nhat Hanh and read him by the mid-sixties. And I felt like I was a Buddhist! In my head, yes, in my heart, too.

I didn't really meet a Buddhist teacher until 1973 when Stan Grof and I went to teach at Naropa Institute. I was practicing meditation by myself and felt like I was a Buddhist in my bones. Then I met Trungpa Rinpoche.

He was just spectacular, but it wasn't the right approach for me. I didn't want that to be my root practice, but I wanted it to be an important stream to feed me because of its emphasis on bodhichitta and the very rich realm of teachings related to death and dying.

The Zen writings I had read felt right for me, just a single practitioner. So when I then met Jack Kornfield in the Seventies, he and I were about the same age, and he recommended a Korean Zen teacher, Seung Sahn. It was a real fit. We practiced together for years. For the first time I had community, a steady meditational practice with others. Finding the iron pivot of the spine even in the midst of great suffering.

Thich Nhat Hanh was my second teacher. I met him in 1985 in Plum Village. We talked of the different ways of manifesting meditation in action and building a world of peace through engaged Buddhism. He inspired me to reduce the complexity of my life and create a refuge of simplicity for myself and others.

Later I had the great fortune of working with Bernie Glassman Roshi, who was my third teacher. He is one who finds gold among the rubble, who takes practice and altars into the streets. The circle of caring and compassion he has opened is ever-expanding, reaching the homeless and the dying and others so often left out or isolated. And I had the great advantage of having friends who were Vipassana teachers, which opened up my appreciation for the sutras and a more methodical approach to the meditational process. People who come here to Upaya are always surprised that I am not so Zen, just throwing people to the wall [laughing with a large chuckle as she says this], and that I try to teach methodically. Step by step, using the widest net possible.

Thirty years later, my practice has developed into what I call Upaya Zen, a Zen that has been really enriched by Mahayana and Vipassana Buddhist teachings as well.

VJD: How has your focus on death and dying become stronger over the past twenty or so years?

JH: My grandmother was my first inspiration in my life, but my work became a lot stronger in 1970 when I was working as a medical anthropologist at the University of Miami Medical School. I saw dying people so marginalized. I saw people's cultural death practices misunderstood or denied. Then Stan Grof and I began doing LSD work with the dying. We saw the psychedelic experience as an opening, a doorway to the transition from living to dying. And I took LSD to accompany the traveler, to learn from and with them. I had a complete and extraordinary immersion in this world of suffering and dying. It is the result of that work, that inspiration, that has carried me for thirty years.

VJD: When I read *The Human Encounter with Death* [by Stanislav Grof and Joan Halifax] it brought back so much of the Sixties, the opening of new paths, the immersion in the unknown. How do you look back on that work now, Roshi Joan?

JH: Oh, it was incredible work, unbelievably profound! And in an incredible time! When I look at the work over the decades with the dying, there is nothing that has been done since that was so brave and so deep. It has been a continual source of learning and inspiration in retrospect.

VJD: When I read that work and think about that time, it has the quality of a carefree child finding the key to a long-locked door.

JH: Well, perhaps, but that's probably because, as Americans, many of us haven't had spiritual traditions in our lives. Oneness with those who have passed on is our spiritual heritage, whether we think of it as the saints in Christianity or the Jewish desert fathers.

It is the heart of Christianity, the very essence of that tradition and Judaism and Islam, too. It is tragic that our world has become so secularized, especially the American life we see now, with the mass culture that overwhelms people.

I never actually felt myself to be a secular person, so now that I am ordained it doesn't seem strange to be separate from the secular world. Since I was little, I always felt like the most important thing was the spiritual life. Even before the age of four I remember that, and the feeling hasn't changed. I've pursued that sense of the importance of the spiritual life without any deviation—really, without ever stopping—since that time.

So I don't think that the word "naïve" applies. I think that some people, perhaps through sickness or karma or something else, develop a sense of spiritual imperative. For other people this develops later in life. Some people wait until they are diagnosed with a disease! You know, a cata-strophic illness impacts one so deeply! I feel blessed to have had a taste from my earliest years. But if I look at someone like Tempe [the Nepalese lama she had just taught with for the first time], he was born into the spir-itual life. He has lived it completely. There are no divisions.

It is a struggle to have a spiritual life in the Western world. The outer world here is based on consuming, and the spiritual world is based on giv-ing away. The materiality of the world holds us back.

VJD: The general feeling of the times has changed so much in that direc-tion. In the past twenty years, it feels as if materialism rules us, as if it rules the whole world. Even if we try individually, it's so hard. But maybe it's always been that way—

JH: Yes, exactly, it always has been that way!

The spiritual life is a choice, you see, a deliberate move away from the material definition of daily life. Humans have always lived with that duality.

But, of course, a lot depends now on how your individual life is. It is certainly easier if you live in a spiritual community. That keeps you active constantly in the spiritual dimension. Working with the dying, you are constantly reminded of what matters: love, kindness, generosity, and our interconnectedness.

But I think it's really hard for people who have to get up early, be at work at nine, who have kids and financial responsibilities. It seems so real that it's really hard to see beyond!

I still struggle with that. I have so many responsibilities that are mate-rial here! I mean, that's why I was sort of begging for *dana* [donations] yesterday. [She laughs and then sighs]. I really hope that people will come here and find meaning, that this will not make it constantly necessary for me to go out and find money and keep this place going the way I have been for the past ten years.

VJD: And yet you have taken on the work of being birth-mother to Upaya. And before that to the Ojai Foundation.

JH: We need mandalas of practice, you know, and I apparently have the constitution to start things. I can get them going. So I start what is needed. I don't know if I have the constitution to sustain them! But I certainly have had the ability to found them, to get institutions moving along that path.

I feel that spiritual centers are essential, critical for everything going on in the world today. Ojai was an educational community deeply influenced by Buddhism and the wilderness, an experiment where teachers and students from different cultures came together to explore what it meant to live a spiritual life. It was an extraordinary experience, a time I lived with porosity, without a real personal life. And then after a decade I needed solitude. I found myself lonely among others. I left Ojai, knowing it had an institutional identity that would stand firm. But I needed to come back to the simple practice of meditation alone.

VJD: And can you speak to the vision process, if that hasn't become too trite a term, to how you came to start this place that you have now for a decade headed? Or the other projects and centers you've started earlier in your life?

JH: Ahh, I just don't understand it! Each time it just happens. Someone will give me something or I'll be in the environment—in a physical situation like it was here at Upaya—and the resources magnetize. This happened before at Ojai, now it's happened at Upaya. Further resources are magnetizing and other situations evolving at this very moment. And my basic nature is to respond, to say, "Yes, I'll do it!" And then I do, I just do.

VJD: So it isn't a vision so much as a response to what life brings?

JH: No, not a vision, not at all! I mean, I never meant to start the Ojai Foundation. And I never meant to start this Zen center. I can't even believe it today. I look back and find it incredible. I didn't set out to do this. And there's a part of me that now feels a little burdened by all the stuff, all the responsibilities that this place demands.

Ojai was an institution that was built from the ground up. We lived in tents, we cooked on fires for so long. I was there ten years, and I did each day exactly that way of building from the ground up. Whatever there was to do, I did it. Whether it was to teach a program or cook a meal or dig a trench, whatever it was, I just did it. That's what a founder does. And after ten years, it simply needed more routinization and I had to leave. Now I am at the same place with this institution. So here I am as the founder at the age of sixty, and it's time to let it go. Have to let it go. I hope to stay here as a teacher, doing what I can for others.

I am at the age now where my commitment is to practice and service, and I want to train successors both for Upaya and for the work with the dying. Getting older is very key here because the enthusiasm for letting go of things increases. I don't have the kind of ambition and energy I had. I really want to use the resources I have now in the best way. And it seems clear that the best way is not to be responsible for all of this. [She opens her arms and gestures toward the windows where we can see Upaya spreading down the hillside.]

VJD: So what would be your hope for the next ten years, assuming that transition you are describing is done?

JH: I don't work that way! I have a hint about what I should do now—which is to do less. Step back a bit. And then I have to see what circumstances come, what the situation needs. It may be a disadvantage but that's how I am, that's who I am. I think a man would make a strategic plan, but I am not a planner like that at all. I live much more in the context, in touch with the situation, trying to respond to what life brings. Not to make it take the shape I want.

VJD: And what about the vision of your death?

JH: I can't think that way! I can't live that way! I don't know what my death will be. I have seen so many people die. I have held so many people as they let go and held them as they struggled and fought and tried to hold on. I hope it will be a good death, a gentle passage, but I can't know that now.

I learn from each death. Issan Dorsey was a teacher for me. We were so close in our work. He was a big tent Buddhist, full of wisdom and not walled in by knowledge. He knew how to care, how to love, and how to help others, those so in need. I went to see him in the hospital. He was so thin, transparent almost. I started to cry. He said, "Please don't cry. It's not necessary."

I had come to him as friend, as a caregiver, but Issan was the bodhisattva. His compassion and love connected us. And suddenly a line from the poet Rainer Maria Rilke was with me: "Love and death are the great gifts that are given to us. Mostly they are passed on unopened."

Life has given me so many gifts, so many people like Issan who live with unconditioned relatedness. Death will be my final teaching, that's all I can know.

VJD: Tell me more about your role as a teacher.

JH: I spend as much time alone as I possibly can. It seems inconceivable to people who only see me as a teacher because I am very present and full of energy, but I am extremely introverted. So I live with this peculiar paradox, being a teacher intensely working with others and yet spending as much time alone as I possibly can. When I am with others I am completely present to the external, engaged in everything there.

I live inside my life. Always, deeply. But I don't think I would have become so invested in meditation if I had been an extrovert. I spend hours every day meditating. And if I were into the social life—well…I mean, I don't socialize. Or as little as I possibly can. And the meditation strengthens me, completely nourishes me.

VJD: So many people seem to come to a spiritual focus as external circumstances drive them there and their pain motivates them. But it sounds for you as though the emergence into Buddhism fit with who you already were, yes?

JH: Right. When I read D.T. Suzuki for the first time, I said, "Oh, I'm one of those!" It wasn't always so easy after, but I felt I'd found my North Star. I've explored so many religions and traditions, both intellectually and experientially, and I feel very comfortable being anything in any tradition, opening to and entering that experience, but my North Star is Buddhism. It has been the pole, the center. And I'm glad I have the enrichment of all these other perspectives.

VJD: It seems the capacity to integrate all these comes from within you, not from an intellectual conviction to bring these together…

JH: Exactly! You thought there was a plan? [She chuckles deeply at this idea.] No, it was much more just life unfolding. I had no idea I would end up in this situation at sixty, and I truly have no idea about my life ten years from now. But I do know that I have dissatisfactions about things now, things that need to be attended to. Turning sixty, sensing this aging beginning now, I have to pace this life I live. I live in a pretty disciplined way, and I am accountable when I find myself tired, just not buoyant for years at a time, then I know something must change in the situation.

VJD: My experience in working with people, especially around questions of aging and dying, is that fear takes hold, where people want "the answer" rather than stepping into darkness. I hope you will teach more about this.

JH: You know, we are all living in a very advantageous time now. A lot of different forces are at play. Major forces. Transition and change are happening in our lives and in our cultures. There is a dissatisfaction with the traditional ways, the old institutional forms, and an opening to finding new approaches. Or integrating ways from the past in what we do now to meet these challenging times.

This makes change in the care of the dying, the whole drama of death and dying, especially open, more than it has even been here in the West. The alienation in the current medical establishment is pushing this. With medicine becoming so mechanized and medical institutions so fiscally-driven and health care professionals finding themselves in situations where their aspirations can't be realized, with all of this going on all at once, there is tremendous disruption in nursing and medicine in general at this time. So change has to come, the forces demand it.

The work with the dying began in the Sixties. We started to challenge the system then. Forty years later there is a more mature relationship to how we care for the dying; it's not the pioneering work that it was then. We have a larger understanding of consciousness and we have the hospice as a vehicle for compassionate caring.

Hospice is now institutionalized to a certain extent, and consciousness is better understood. And the discipline of palliative care has been well established—and we want it! We have seen so many hard deaths, and we have learned from that. So palliative care now is a team approach and based in a vision of compassion, relieving suffering, not curing.

And I think that people involved in spiritual practice have now been doing it for some time. They have ten, twenty, even thirty or forty years under their belts. They have a more mature relationship with practice, and they bring that to the whole field, the care of the dying and the process of change that has to happen now. So I think the timing is really excellent for compassionate care of dying people and growing understanding of the importance of preparation for death.

Now is a better time than any other era, at least in the decades I've been involved with this work. There's been no more advantageous time for change. This is a time when conventionally and traditionally-trained health care professionals—physicians and nurses as well as social workers and hospice staff—are seeking to re-infuse this work and their own lives with meaning. Dying people are reaching out, asking for the spiritual dimension to be offered as a part of caring, not simply and solely the medical.

This process has been going on for decades, I think. It's a slow maturation but a wonderful ripening now. The kinds of people I work with are mostly very conventional, and most of them are not Buddhist practitioners or interested in Buddhism; they are simply reaching for the spiritual. I get phone calls from all over the world from people asking for help and guidance about this. Good time is spent on this. And I know Ram Dass is being called like this too, is responding in the same way. And even though we can't actually be there, we are still attending to people who have realized the spiritual dimension to life and to death. This is of utmost importance. Life by life, death by death, how we live and die is being transformed. The deep roots have grown. This is such a time of enormous change, a time building for decades to spiritually embrace living and dying.

VJD: And do you see this making it possible for East and West to find understanding and peace? Having lived in the Middle East and still having family there, I can hardly watch the news now, seeing the suffering.

JH: When the light is really bright, the shadow is really deep. And right now the shadow is very, very deep.

And yet there are extraordinary people in the world working for change. I see so many extraordinary young people who understand the past and are moving forward. Like Britt Olson, a young physician who will lead in practicing medicine with spiritual depth.

There are so many young people who are just inspiring, intelligent, and committed. And they will make this transformation, I know that. More than any other time in our history, I think the possibility for peace and a compassionate caring world is here. We're moving out of a flowering, a starting, toward something becoming substantial. Whether it is the amazing impact of the four-part series "A Death of One's Own" that Bill Moyers produced for PBS [September, 2000] or palliative care or the number of institutions engaged in complementary or alternative medical approaches and utilizing the work that I've developed over the past thirty years on death and dying. It's all just part of the curriculum now. It's no longer a rare thing!

There are not so many people who have a lifetime of experience in this area. Ram Dass is one, Frank Ostaseski is another, there are a few more. But there are young people who actually have realized as much as we have in less than a decade. So we pioneers can kind of kick back and look at the young people who are coming up, those who have really excellent spiritual training as well as medical or nursing background and commitment, and now they are in institutions and it's happening.

VJD: Any last thoughts you want to leave people with?

JH: I feel truly positive about the progress of human life across the world, the changes going on now. And you know, my own life has been nothing but obstacles, and yet I look at obstacles as nothing other than opportunities. The spiritual life is what it is. Since human beings began making those strange markings on the caves until now, the longing hasn't changed. The spiritual struggles remain. Our ability to recognize this is increasing actually. Buddhist ideas are now seen as congruent with ideas in science. So there is more link, more consistency between these worlds that people had seen as separate. What gives me hope is the understanding that all life is interconnected. Life and death intertwined, this gives me hope for us all as we live, as we die, always moving into the unknown.

Thich Nhat Hanh
With Each Breath, We Continue Forever

"Buddhism must not be just theory. It must come from real experience, and it must work to relieve suffering."

"My body is not mine alone but a long continuation of my mother and my father, my grandparents and my ancestors. Together, we were leaving footprints in the damp soil."

THICH NHAT HANH lives on a hillside far up in the grape vine and sunflower covered tracts of the Dordogne region in southwest France in a place called Plum Village, a Vietnamese Zen Buddhist retreat center he founded in 1982. "Thây," as he is called by his students, was teaching at the yearly summer retreat when I came to speak with him in mid-July of 2003. A tradition for more than two decades now, this month-long intensive retreat offers the opportunity to study and live Buddhism, and it draws participants from around the world and of every age, from young children to elders.

Thich Nhat Hanh founded Plum Village after instituting centers of study in the East and the West. He was born in central Vietnam in 1926. Sixteen years later, he took monk's vows. Over the next two decades he founded the first Buddhist high school in his country, published several books on Buddhism and others of poetry, helped to initiate Van Hanh Buddhist University in Saigon, and articulated the principles of "engaged Buddhism" as his country writhed within the prolonged war that engulfed north and south.

He first came to the U.S. in 1961. He studied religion and taught Buddhism at Columbia University. Three years later he returned to his country only to be branded "traitor" by all sides in the bloody conflict. In 1966, he was exiled to France and later founded a Buddhist community near Paris called Sweet Potatoes. Although he has petitioned the Vietnamese government several times since the peace in 1973, he has not been allowed to return. His efforts to promote world peace have been tireless over the past fifty years, and he was nominated for the Nobel Peace Prize by Dr. Martin Luther King, Jr. He has written over twenty books including the best-sellers *Being Peace* (1987), *Teachings on Love* (1998), *Living Buddha, Living Christ* (1995), and *Anger* (2001).

Living in Plum Village for a week, we all waited for the sun to set and the thermometer to fall. Yet Thây seemed untouched by the heat, the myriad of morning to evening activities, and the pressures of speaking to hundreds who gathered to hear him each day. His face had a bright glow each morning as he entered the hall. He kept that same incandescent quality during this long conversation in the afternoon summer sun.

VJD: You told a story yesterday that has stuck with me, about the Buddha at the end of his life. His followers said no to a person coming to see him, saying that the Buddha was dying and must be left in peace. But the Buddha intervened, welcoming the person and teaching him until his very last breath. That story seems very apt for your life as a Buddhist monk and a teacher and spiritual leader of so many people. How did this all begin?

TNH: We are born to continue. For us in Vietnam there was no going to look for Buddhism because Buddhism was inside us all. Always. Our ancestors have always practiced Buddhism, and we were born to continue that practice. There is truly no searching, no finding, nothing to do. Just a continuation.

VJD: Is this true for those of us in the West as well?

TNH: Yes, you don't have to go East, you don't have to go West. You just continue!

But the circumstances and the environment may help to touch off something. In Vietnam generations after generations have practiced Buddhism and this brings out the sense of continuation very strongly. But from time to time there is a kind of encounter that can also bring this out very strongly. For me, it was the war in Vietnam.

I learned recently that in California there are certain pine trees that require heat to reproduce. The seeds are only released by very intense heat and then they burst open. War is like that. Maybe a seed that has been transmitted by our ancestors needs some kind of very strong heat in order to burst out and to sprout and become a new tree. That is why I said this morning that sometimes suffering helps create the conditions of change.

It is like a piece of iron that needs a lot of heating to become a sword. Suffering plays an important role in helping the spiritual to be reborn, to manifest. This is why we speak of engaged Buddhism; it is the kind of Buddhism that can really offer the answers to difficult situations.

I was born in a country where colonialism, social injustice, political oppression, poverty, and war were all happening at same time! So as a young person I was eager to look for a way out. And learning from history, you know that your ancestors in ancient times were able to lead the country out of difficult situations through their Buddhist practice.

As a young person, I gained great confidence by digging very deeply and finding a kind of Buddhism that helped me and gave me the conviction that there was a way out of the situation. I was able to maintain that conviction, that deep desire that kept me alive. Otherwise I would have been assaulted or I would have surrendered to other kinds of temptations. Temptations not in terms of wealth or fame or beautiful women or power, but temptations like communism. Communism was very tempting because I saw that many communists really sacrificed their lives hoping to build a better social system. They were ready to die for a vision of liberation.

At the same time, I saw that many Buddhists practiced in a way that was so separate from the suffering in the society around them. This is something like the criticism I hear in the West of Christianity now. The Church is not always responding enough to the suffering around it. It is not providing the younger generation with appropriate ways to practice. The Church is living in a vacuum.

VJD: Their ideals aren't lived in the real world?

TNH: They don't have practices to work for social justice, equality and so on. And it was the same for me as a young person when I looked at the kind of Buddhism around me. I thought, this kind of Buddhism cannot do anything to help, but if I dig deeper, I will discover something.

That kind of intention and conviction helped me to continue. It brought me deeper and helped me not to fall back into so many of the temptations that existed then.

And that is why we invented what is called "engaged Buddhism." It was born from our conviction that Buddhism must not be just theory. It must come from real experience, and it must work to relieve suffering.

VJD: Sister Chân Không spoke yesterday about the work in the countryside during these years, how relieving suffering and facilitating change must flow together.

TNH: Yes, doing work like that, the work that defined "engaged Buddhism." We were not satisfied with just talking about Buddhism or preaching its precepts. It must be real experience, work connected with the teaching. We practiced engaged Buddhism across the country. We went to slums, we went to the countryside. We went into the war itself. We saved wounded children, we buried dead bodies, we brought food, medicine, shelter. And we died! Many of us died during that time, hundreds of us served and died. And we really created engaged Buddhism with our lives, not just our ideas.

In the West now there is also the idea of engaged Buddhism as an instrument of social change. And Buddhists in other countries in the East have also have had the same ideas and the same desire. In Sri Lanka, Thailand, Burma—all through the East! Of course it is a minority who hold this idea, but the hope of engaged Buddhism as an instrument of social change is a very strong one, very deep.

And for me...well, instead of going East, I went West. And the encounter with the West helps a lot because there is a lot of suffering in the West. A lot! You will see in Asia that although there are many poor countries, the people don't suffer that much. They may suffer from a lack of food or shelter or social justice, but even when they are very poor they can laugh and enjoy life a lot.

But here in the West, especially in America, the suffering is enormous, especially the suffering in people's minds. Also there is so much suffering from broken families, alcoholism, mental illness—it's a lot, oh, a lot! And when you encounter that kind of suffering, you cannot offer the kind of Buddhism that has nothing to do with it. You cannot engage people in practicing a kind of Buddhism that just helps them forget the actual situation or move away from it for a short while.

VJD: So spirituality is not about escaping reality?

TNH: Yes, it can not be just escapism. Of course, escaping may help from time to time, but only in small ways and only with a few people who can buy such an escape. The majority of people cannot escape, they must continue to fight. That is why the kind of Buddhism we offer at Plum Village helps us to restore strength and face reality in its totality. And learn to face it not just as isolated individuals but as a Sangha, a community.[1] To face suffering fully, yes, and to face it as a part of a Sangha. As a Sangha, we are each stronger. That is why we make a lot of effort in sangha-building, making the Sangha an institution for helping individual suffering.

So going West has been very helpful for me. And if we from the East have succeeded to some extent in helping our Western brothers and sisters to learn, we have also then inspired people in Asia. When we go to China, Korea, Japan, and other parts of Asia, people are very interested in what we have to say because we have succeeded to some extent in offering and sharing the practice of Buddhism in the West. They say, "Oh, if *Westerners* succeed in transforming their suffering because of the practice of engaged Buddhism, then we can do it too!" So they get more confidence in their own tradition.

It's funny, but what happens in Europe and America has a very good effect on Asia as far as learning and practicing Buddhism is concerned. When I visited the Minister of Cultural Affairs in China, I told him about what were doing in Europe and America. He was very surprised to learn that so many Westerners were interested in Buddhism and that many have even become monks and nuns. This was very strange to him because he thought that he understood Buddhism. But the kind of Buddhism that he had learned is not the same kind that we practice. So he...oh, he kind of thought about this, and he told me he would go back and learn Buddhism again. He thought that there must be something really good in Buddhism for Westerners to be interested like that!

VJD: So Buddhism is journeying East and journeying West at the same time!

TNH: It seems that going West is at the same time going East. When you go West you are also going East and going East is also going West, both at the same time. For me that is the best thing—so funny but true!

VJD: This morning you spoke of the great suffering you see here in France, the teenagers committing suicide, increasing violence, so many problems. And it seems to me that so much has to do with our great fears of dying.

How do you experience growing older in the West?

TNH: I think I am growing younger and younger instead of growing older and older. If you look at me, you see that!

I feel younger and younger each day. Truly. I do not feel the disintegration of this body means my end because I am able to see me, see me alive in very young forms all around me, living a little bit everywhere. I have invested myself in so many people who are now the continuation of me as I am the continuation of those before me. So I have confidence in myself and yet I don't consider this body is me. The disintegration of this body doesn't affect me.

I truly practice nonself. This is the heart of my practice. If you look deeply you see yourself in your son, your daughter, your disciples, and your friends. They can continue you very well. So why think about your ending? Every effort of your daily life is to invest in the younger generations.

The Buddha did the same. He continued teaching for forty-five years after enlightenment and he transmitted himself in this way to generations of disciples for all those forty-five years. And his death in the present moment did not touch him. If you are free in your seeing, you can still recognize him around us in different forms. So the Buddha never dies.

The Buddha is becoming younger and younger all the time. We are each the continuation of the Buddha. So why should we not do this too?

Buddhists talk about nonself and no-birth, no-death. But we don't really practice this each day. Meditation is to practice this in order to see your true nature, to know no-birth, no-death, to know each moment there is no coming, no going. This is the cream of the Buddhist teaching and practice.

If you are not able to touch your nature of no-birth, no-death, you have not completely succeeded in your Buddhist practice. If you practice Buddhism to get some relief from your suffering, yes, that is OK. But then you have to go further. The greatest relief that you get from Buddhist practice is to go beyond the notion of birth and death, to overcome birth and death, overcome notions of beginning and ending, of still thinking that you are going to die, that your life only lasts eighty years or 100 years. If this is so, you haven't learned Buddhism fully.

Our lives are like waves in the ocean. The wave might be scared if she conceives of herself as having a beginning and an end, of going up and then going down. But if the wave recognizes that she is water—not only is she a wave but she is also water—in that moment when she recognizes herself as water, there is no fear left. Being water you are no longer afraid of going back, going down, into the all. There is no beginning, no end; there is no up and no down for the water.

So I don't consider anything a success except that knowing. Until that point, I don't consider a Buddhist practitioner to have success. You can build something, you can produce something, okay. Perhaps you will even become famous. But you will not feel truly at peace, you will not truly have success, unless you realize no-birth, no-death.

That is why I don't need to die in order to be reborn. You see that I have been reborn in many, many forms. And I can see myself out of myself. This is the teaching of Buddhism: to see your body outside of your body, to step beyond the forms. And that is the moment that you have really seen your true body, not just the shape you take to live, to be.

VJD: Yes, this has great meaning for me.

TNH: I think the suffering in the West as well as in the East lies in the fact that people are looking for happiness in the direction of wealth, power, fame, and sex. And if they have the time to look around, they will see that many people have a lot of these—a lot of power, a lot of wealth and sex and fame—but they still suffer very deeply. They even commit suicide.

But there is happiness here too. I have met a lot of people who have experienced true, deep enduring happiness. This is not a product of power or money or sex or fame. You can have a lot of money, but within yourself you can be empty. If you have understanding and love within yourself, you can be happy. Even if you live very simply in terms of lodging, food, and shelter. If you have a lot of understanding and love inside and give others understanding and love, then you are a happy person.

So the way out of suffering is for us to wake up, to look for happiness in the direction of understanding and love. There are spiritual paths to do this. And that is why I have said over and over that this new century should be spiritual—it must be spiritual—or there will be no century at all. Some politicians are bringing a spiritual dimension into their lives, not a rigidness about religion, but a spirituality. All political and business leaders must bring a spiritual dimension into their lives. Otherwise they will destroy their lives and ours. They will destroy us as a world as well.

Without a spiritual life these people suffer a lot. If they have a spiritual life, they will suffer less and they will serve better. That is really the dream of engaged Buddhism. It is not just talk, it is about how we actually live our lives, each day, each moment.

This is very important when working with the dying. If a person has lived this practice, they can inspire a lot of peace and non-fear in the dying person. Because non-fear can be transferred. When we are living non-fear, there are so many things that we can transfer to a person who is ill or dying. If you have seen there is no end of life, that life will continue always, then you can show that to the dying person. You live it. Your life proves that to the dying person. And he will die smiling, she will die without fear, smiling with acceptance at the last breath.

VJD: Your book *No Death, No Fear* has taught me so much about dying. Before beginning this book project I spent weeks writing about death and loss in my own life, particularly about my mother's long suffering and my life after her death. In your book you describe your own mother's death and how it was one year before the pain eased.

TNH: Yes. I experienced her presence as I walked on the hillside behind a temple. Each time my foot touched the ground, I felt her presence. And I knew my body was not mine alone but a long continuation of my mother and my father, my grandparents and my ancestors. Together we were leaving footprints in the damp soil.

VJD: Do you have any last words you want to share?

TNH: Just this. We are born to continue. Mindful with each step, mindful with each breath, we continue forever.

---

1 A Sangha is a community of practice, a group of people who practice Buddhism together.

Michael Eigen
Strengthening Our Emotional Muscles

"It's part of the paradox of living that keeping the long view in mind enables one to be in the here and now."

MICHAEL EIGEN is a psychologist and psychoanalyst with a private practice in Manhattan. He teaches in the Postdoctoral Program in Psychotherapy and Psychoanalysis at New York University and is Senior Member of the National Psychological Association for Psychoanalysis. He has written many books that bring differing intellectual traditions together in dynamic and unique ways, including *Psychic Deadness,* (1996), *The Psychoanalytic Mystic* (1998), Ecstasy (2001) and *Rage* (2002). He has described himself as a "Jewish Buddhist psychological mystic." He focuses on the change and transformations that occur when individuals are faced with pain, crisis, and death.

On a clear Saturday morning in late November, 2003, I found my way onto the busy Brooklyn street where Michael Eigen lives with his wife and two boys. He welcomed me warmly, bringing me tea. We sat on the large wood kitchen table amid his books and papers. He has a warm smile and his eyes sparkled as he spoke with a contagious enthusiasm.

Victoria Jean Dimidjian: One thing that stands out about your work is how you've woven spirituality into psychology, specifically as it relates to aging and dying. Was there anything in your growing up that influenced this work?

Michal Eigen: I grew up in Passaic, New Jersey but I could see the city across the water, just vaguely, just the skyline. When I was a little boy I said to myself, When I'm big, I'm going to go there. And soon I played hooky and came to the city to see singers and bands. I saw all kinds of singers and bands. Big bands still played in theaters. I saw Charlie Parker and Miles [Davis] and Bud Powell at Birdland. After college and a number of false starts, I finally managed to move to New York City permanently.

VJD: You've written that it was then you were exposed to Buddhism. What opened that door?

ME: I turned on to Buddhism in my last year in college at the University of Pennsylvania in 1957. There was a poet—who's no longer a poet actually—the last time I met him he was a stock market investor—how can a poet no longer be a poet, is that possible? Bob Williamson. He told me to read *Mysticism: Christian and Buddhist*[1], and I loved it.

That was my beginning contact with Buddhism. Unfortunately, it had a terrible effect on me because I stopped going to classes and sat out on the lawn, but it was too late to stop me from graduating! When I was a sophomore or junior, my roommate told me what his therapist said about his dreams. The therapist, Henry Elkin, was trained in Zurich, a Jungian. And when I heard the dream interpretations, bells just rang. It was like falling in love, and I've been in love with dreams ever since. When I graduated, I looked Henry up and started therapy with him from three to five days a week.

VJD: Many of us who lived through the Sixties have tried to fuse wisdom from the East with Western psychology. You have combined more separate aspects than almost anyone.

ME: Well, I've tried! But they are pretty splattered!

I began my contact with Eastern ideas while in college. I saw Suzuki Roshi in Philadelphia, maybe around 1956–57. There are cases when a little contact with someone can have a big effect and this was one of them. When someone asked him a question about passivity he said, "Passivity, what's wrong with passivity?" And proceeded to say good things about the passive pleasures he gets.

Once my contact with Eastern "ideas" began, it never ended. I would rather use the word "experience" than "idea." It was experiential for me from the outset. It hit me through and through.

Once the original face hit, well, it's something that's continued all my life. Really it started in the end of the Fifties. Knowing the Beat poets in New York. I went off to Mexico and then up to San Francisco. Met Allen Ginsberg, heard him read *Howl* in 1958, I think. Now my kid just bought his late poems. Some of them are really terrific.

VJD: So that was part of your growing up, the Beats and the Eastern influences in the Fifties?

ME: I'm still a Beat analyst! I tried to learn whatever I could, getting tastes from all of it. I sat in meditation with many teachers. My organizational compass was probably Taoism, but I didn't know any Taoists, mostly Hindus and Buddhists.

I really don't try to do anything except to stick with what is coming up at the time. I just try to make contact with what is there at the moment. I've never tried to integrate anything. I'm not a theorist.

VJD: So exploration of spiritual traditions have been ways of helping you be more in the moment?

ME: Yes...or to evolve, to let that continue and evolve, not to die in any final way.

VJD: And is that evolution part of your family too?

ME: Yes, but it's a mixed tradition. I am a first generation American on my father's side. He came over from Vienna after the First World War. My mother's father came a little later from Poland. She was born here on the Lower East Side. She spoke Yiddish before she spoke English. And my father always said that he refused to learn English in schools in Vienna because he didn't want to have an accent. So he learned it when he got here—and he didn't have an accent.

But my family, on both sides, had elements steeped in a sacred tradition. A rabbi would come once a year to our home for donations. There was something about him I loved but didn't understand. I always looked forward to his coming. It wasn't till decades later that I understood he carried a sense of the holy. He shined with a sense of the holy. Now I have words for the light in and around his face, his glow, his halo. My father would drop everything when he came.

My father, though, lived a secular life throughout my childhood, mainly focused on making a living. My mother kept kosher until her mother died when I was maybe four or five—she did it mainly so that her mother could come and eat with us, but now I wonder. I went to *shul* on weekends and tried to get my father to go but he preferred sleeping late. Later in his life he *davened* [prayed] and chanted the *haftorahs* [a portion of the prophets sung after the main Torah reading]. The fall before he died, he chanted the Yom Kippur haftorah—the story of Jonah—in the immigrant shul downtown in Passaic, where he went as a teen with his father, who lost a leg on the boat over. It was a difficult life, filled with beauty. Both parents emphasized goodness, doing good. My father would say, "God means good."

I had two early spiritual experiences. The first was when I was two and my father carried me to the hospital to get an appendix operation. And it was late and I looked up and saw the stars. I was blown away. I couldn't believe anything like that existed. I didn't know what I was seeing and I asked my father and he tried to explain, they were stars. Was it milk coming at me? What kind of light is this? They were outside me but they were like shimmering crystal inside me. Light inside resonates with light outside and perhaps the reverse is true as well. All trauma and depression fell away and I was lifted to the stars.

The second time it happened was hearing a clarinet player. There was a beggar in the Catskills, you know, once known as the borscht belt, who came around playing Yiddish music. And it made my spine tingle and everything lit up. And I said, "Gee, I want to do that." I got a clarinet within the year and played and played for many years. When my clarinet teacher played a song as my reward after a lesson, I laughed and laughed.

The next super-amazing joy kernel was when I was sixteen or seventeen, kissing a girl named Laurel good night. It was the same as the stars and the clarinet music but with soft lips, melding body, heart feeling. I jumped and danced and shouted and skipped and flew all the way home. Still, consciousness of the light as such came later. A lot more pain came, too.

VJD: What was that like?

ME: One of the earlier moments came from being on a bus when I was twenty. I was in a lot of pain, not able to breathe and I passed out. I was in intense emotional pain, doubled over, entirely into the pain, more and more absorbed by it, and then had an unexpected opening to the light. The pain was gone, absorbed by the light. The light was precious. It was a hard experience but one of the great things about living. The pain was real, the light was real. In time I would get to know more about what I was going through, but living it was more important.

VJD: If, as you say, we shouldn't take the cookbook approach to healing, how do we fully accept the difficulty, the pain?

ME: I don't know if acceptance is the right word. It's more stick-to-itiveness. In our society we have a hyper-consciousness relating to bodies and so much emphasis on physical muscles. Well, now we're in danger of losing our emotional muscles. As soon as a kid is brought in to see a psychiatrist, within half an hour he's on medication. There's no chance for people to see what they can do. No time to interact with another, to use their internal resources.

So I think there may be a growing loss of the capacity to cope, a growing failure to develop and explore psychic resources, and especially a loss of ability to use or even have much of a chance to use one's emotional self. So it's not so much about acceptance as use, just sticking with emotions, however painful.

Our ability to stay with it varies. One moment you are with your emotional sensor up to a point, then you lose it, then it's back and you use it some more. You stick with it and then it gets away again, almost a kind of rhythm, back and forth. Being there, not being there, coming back again. Breakdown, recovery, breakdown, recovery. Losing, finding, losing, finding. Maybe there is understanding and acceptance as part of the background brew but what's more important is somehow letting the rhythm lead, finding that rhythm, even jump-starting it if necessary.

I don't think feelings get digested today. There are massive social pressures to thin feelings out or eject them like missiles at or into others. Feelings get commercialized, politically marshaled and packaged, turned into money or power, slicked up. Various electronic media and image producing machines speed and spread the resulting packages and programs, so that feelings are used for gain.

What's needed now more than anything is a worldwide working emotional digestive system. If that could evolve, our feelings for ourselves and each other could evolve too. They go together, our feelings for life, for each other, and unconscious life that can support them.

VJD: Sometime back, you said in an interview that when it came to social and economic inequalities of the world, you were more of a Buddhist. Do you still feel that way?

ME: No! Well, yes and no! I will always be a Buddhist in a deep, deep sense. Buddhism helps mediate the possibility of just being there with your thoughts and feelings without holding on to them, letting them come and go, not stopping them. That's deeply important to me. Always will be. But I'm also interested in holding them up, looking at them, seeing what they are made of. There are Buddhist texts that go into all these details, taking apart the skeleton of the psyche.

Buddhism fortifies you. It helps you to think about yourself: thinking, well, this is what I am thinking now, but that could cause a lot of harm. Why not wait a few seconds and see how it looks? See how different the self looks in just a few seconds. From that point of view, if Bush could do that, if Osama could do that, if Saddam, if all kinds of fanatics could do that, what a change.

VJD: But what about the rage these people, and all of us, have? You recently wrote a book with this title.

ME: In *Rage* I focus on workings of destructiveness that block our evolution. Rage is so very prevalent in our lives. Not just road rage, which

Oedipus displayed, murdering the stranger in his path, the stranger at the crossroads. Rage is ruining lives. Rage ruins relationships and damages one's own self.

Look at the repercussions spreading across the globe!

While I feel that the focus starts with oneself, I do feel now more of a need to speak out, to say something about what is happening as it impacts me and others, as it impacts our world, the life we share together. I am still dedicated to the changing moment, the living moment, and the next, and the next. But I also feel more involved with peoples' plights across the world and our own at home. I think it a sin not to speak out at this point, as it would be something like remaining silent in Germany in the Thirties. My faith, my hope is that we are involved in a world group process in which we gradually correct and add to each other. Time will tell if this is wish or reality.

Maybe all of us should say we don't know what to do next. Those leaders so intent on war should all say, "I don't know what to do next!" If we keep on saying that and kept trying to act from not-knowing rather than knowing it all, if we did that, everything would be very different.

VJD: Yes, it is frightening that the world perceives our country as thinking it knows what to do, and most of the world fears that.

ME: Such hubris. Such a destructive omniscience!

But we're not the only guilty ones. The Palestinians aren't innocent of this, not any more than Israelis. There's no innocence in this. It is a human co-responsibility.

VJD: You've said that your life's work is working with individuals in pain, opening up that pain, being with them in that pain. It would seem to me that the next step from suffering would be passage into compassion, but for the most part the next step seems to be into rage. Why is that?

ME: Maybe you have a picture of us, all of us humans now, as being more evolved than we really are. Maybe what's now at stake is our evolving to the point where we can cushion pain with compassion. But that capacity has to evolve individually and collectively. Sometimes pain has meaning. It tells one something is off, that one's way of life is hurting. Often violence or anger is an attempt to make the pain of one's life go away. But the pain doesn't go away, it gets worse.

In our old brain and autonomic nervous system we are programmed to blot out pain with rage. At least that is one of our programs, to react to pain or loss of control with anger. Rage and outrage rail against the pain, try to make the pain go away, blot it out, destroy it. It may cause a lot of psychic damage trying to end the pain. Rage does not solve the problem of pain. Not anymore than murder solves tribal enmity. But we do keep trying to murder pain away. That's where therapy comes in.

VJD: On an individual level, oh yes! But what about on a species level?

ME: Well, I'm an inveterate hoper! And I do think great things are coming. We've already shown ourselves we can destroy life. We have all kinds of ways to do that. Destructive alternatives are everywhere. We're terrific at murder, but we're not so terrific at peaceful alternatives, helping, easing the pain. There are many for whom helping does not provide enough punch. We have to find ways to make peace fiercely attractive enough, to find peaceful ways that satisfactorily support intensity and enable intensity to be nourishing.

But there are increasing numbers of people who want to help, who know their own pain and want to ease suffering. It's a race to the masses now. Maybe there are or will be as many helping as destroying, maybe more. Maybe the helpers will reach a critical mass and tip the balance. It's essential to mobilize the caring instinct.

Unfortunately, the destructive impulses seem to have control of the media, of popular culture. So many movies, TV programs, ersatz violence, making violence fascinating, unreal. Or all too real, yet hideously attractive. As if curiosity is wedded to destruction rather than sex and generative aspects of living. Perhaps there is a sense in which people feel destroyed in some important, elusive ways and find ways to stare at and reproduce or magnify this sense of destruction. As if curiosity has little left to be curious about except death, and even that has become boring. Even at this point we can act on a personal level since, and I think this is something Buddhism teaches, it is possible to face anything. And in a way, literally impossible as it is, it is necessary to face everything.

VJD: That brings me to asking about your reflections on time and aging, Mike, as you move through your sixties—

ME: Soon seventies! I'm sixty-seven now.

VJD: You've written about aging and the dying of family members and those close to you. As someone now entering the last stage of life, what are your thoughts on impermanence?

ME: That's a very complex topic. I work with dying people now and sick people facing the end of their life, even a couple of younger people facing the end of their life. They are a small part of my practice, but a significant number. The topic is close to me. I've written only about one of these clients so far [in *The Electrified Tightrope* and in *Psychic Deadness.*] I called him "Smith." He was dying of heart disease and he came to me so he could die better. He felt he had lived a lie. In our work he made contact with what he called the lie. Doing that gave him a sense of being at one with himself.

I am doing some writing now about a woman who was diagnosed with a fatal disease three years ago. She did not expect to be alive this long but we are still together. In fact, she's gotten much better and has not needed a transfusion in over a year. She had been getting them weekly and doctors feared her body would eventually stop responding. She's a woman of great faith and perhaps needed a place for her faith to find a rich soil.

As I've gotten older, my practice has gotten older with me. I have seen a lot of patients a long time. Some have been with me thirty years! I don't think it is good to rush. There is too much emphasis on speed now. Some people need long-term contact. There is so much damage that they need a supportive bond that can go on a very long time, sometimes the rest of their lives. I think it cruel to deny people this kind of contact if they need it. A shorter but telling variation of this happens with children. The mother who takes her son out of therapy because, "He is getting dependent on you." Well, I've always wondered. What is wrong with that? You want him dependent on drugs, on medication, on your absence, on your controlling presence? What is wrong with being dependent on another human being as long as that is really needed and useful?

Someone who specializes in short-term therapy recently consulted me. When she heard from another person about how long some people work with me she said, "They should sue him!" [He laughs and shakes his head.] She believes in getting them in and out the door. Not like me.

VJD: And your reflections on death?

ME: I'm not as afraid of death as I should be. I used to be terrified of death when I was younger. It dawned on me very early that I would die because I saw my uncle and another man carry my grandmother out of her house when she died. I was under five. When I was twenty-one, my ten year old brother got killed, run over by a truck, and this was devastating. During my teens I had acute terror of dying. I had friends who became suicidal, depressed over this kind of terror. I wasn't depressed over it, over my certain death, but I was scared, very anxious. Hyper-anxious. Maybe one reason I see patients so long a time is to undo my brother's death, or forestall death, as well as make life better.

As I entered my twenties, I did not expect that fear to go away. I said, "Okay, if that's the way it is, I'll live with it." But it did go away. And that was kind of miraculous. It went away in an instant. It was when I was with my Aunt Bert when she was dying. I was visiting her in the hospital. I was holding her hand, and she was telling me how bitter she was, how she didn't expect this to happen, how it took her by surprise. I was just sitting, holding her hand, listening. And I looked at her and suddenly something happened. I couldn't feel where life left off and death began. It was an experience, not a thought. It just happened. Suddenly, I felt there wasn't much of a difference somehow. It wasn't a feeling against death, not against life, not for either of them. It was just the sense that I had somehow entered a transitional space where there were no boundaries.

You know, Freud made the remark that he wouldn't be surprised if there wasn't such a great caesura between pre-birth and post-birth life as people were making out; there wasn't such a big gap in pre- and post-birth consciousness as we thought. And that's what I felt that day. And suddenly that terror was gone. I'd been through all that analysis, looking at this and that. And this experience wasn't anything analytic. It was just looking at my dying aunt, hearing her express her fears, her anger, just staying there and holding her hand. And all of a sudden all my fears were gone, they all fluttered into another realm.

And I've been relieved of the fear of death ever since! That pretty much sucked the fear right out of me. I mean, I'm not eager to die, but it's not something I fear. I've come to feel as my father did, that death is part of the natural cycle of things.

VJD: So much is written about the vision of a good death these days, what do you think of the concept?

ME: My father had a good death, my mother had a bad death. My father's death was what turned me on to Judaism as an adult. I had a Jewish streak but I really became a Jew through my father's death. I used to go and visit him in the hospital about once a week. I brought this, brought that to him. And one day I went up there, and there was my sister, and my mother, so we were all there. And then our rabbi came in. He'd been out of town. And my sister had been angry at him because he hadn't come recently. But now he was there.

He sang the *sh'ma*, part of *adom olam*, gave the priestly blessing—bits that said, "Don't be afraid, give yourself to God," basically. That's what I was trying to say before, how I would say to God, "Who am I to say what you have done? Why put death in the world? I wouldn't have done it that way. I would have tried something else, you know! But you did it, it's done." So given that, we make the best of it. And so much radiance grows out of that. But even this kind of translation and re-phrasing doesn't come close to the actual moment.

Before the rabbi was done I became aware my father passed away. Passed peacefully. He had waited for that. He couldn't say it, he was in a coma. But when the words were said, he could go. He was lovely. He looked perfect. He had a germ of the holiness that I valued so much, that I could see in holy ones since I was a child.

So then the rabbi left and he didn't know my father died while he was singing and we didn't tell him. Something of the experience as I had with my Aunt Bert came to me then. Except as my father passed away, almost to the moment, the words came to me in an authoritative, moving way, "The Lord of Abraham, Isaac and Jacob lives." This was a very clear, surprising and full experience, moving and compelling and inviting. A little while later—to my wife's horror—I went through an Orthodox phase. The night of my father's funeral I began going to shul and soon began studying with the sons of the *rebbe* whose holy glow touched me in childhood. They were still alive, old men now, in Brooklyn, not far from where I lived. My contact with mystical Judaism deepened. My orthodox phase is now gone, thank God, but it was beautiful while it lasted. But really too much for me and my family. My life couldn't support it. My wife's common sense saw us through.

VJD: And do you see yourself as you age more intensely focused on what comes next?

ME: No. Just being, just being there. Being in touch with what life, nature, God, spirit— whatever words we use—whatever has seen fit to put us through this mill. To fully live the constellation of my life. Not to be too horrible with my kids. To keep trying to be better with people.

VJD: As your work with people at the end of life, are there sources of support you give to them?

ME: I haven't been able to figure this out mostly. Only one is religious in a semi-traditional way. She moved from Catholicism to Judaism with a good dose of Eastern understanding, too. She couldn't do Buddhist meditation because her psyche would persecute her while sitting. She could not sit. Things would come she feared would destroy her. It was too terrifying. Her body could not take it. Prayer is better for her. She needs contact with a personal Other. Not everyone can handle moving deep inside and there are different ways to do it.

VJD: How do we do this?

ME: Well, you give it your best shot! It's hard to find the right terms for this. Funny how things come around. Jesus said, "Wherever two are, I'll be there. I'll be the third." I suppose to me that's meant the Holy Spirit as the third between people, the link that uplifts, bringing people to new places.

We all have a feeling, a sense there must be something else. I'm not just the sum of my predatory impulses, the so-called old brain, autonomic pulls. I'm not even reducible to high-brain thoughts, the smart know-it-all stuff. We keep thinking and feeling there is something else, there must be something else. It used to be called "essence." But now that's not popular. So what can there be? The voice of the prophets still insists we are all sinners. And Holden Caulfield is there saying, "Adults are phoney." There's that feeling, that voice: there must be something else.

No one likes Jeremiah these days because he's so glum, but he has a passage where he talks about this. He says, "Don't follow your heart. Don't follow your eyes. They get you into trouble. They'll lead you astray. What you are looking for is something else, somewhere else. It's not your heart. It's not the beloved your eyes can see." He seems to want to say it's the voice of God you are looking for but how does he do that? He can't find the words. Finally, he gives up. Almost in exasperation he blurts out, "It's a burning!" [He shouts out the phrases.] It's a burning inside you! A burning inside you that gives you another heart!"

That's his shot at it. Not half-bad either.

There is a way that this voice speaks in Judaism, heart burning its way to a new heart. There are ways it does this in Catholicism, in Buddhism… In Islam, Sufis have pulled out a thread from the Koran as a way to make a direct connection that embraces all beings. In any of these traditions, threads are there to make a connection with what we all value most. For me, this is less a Buddhist thing or a Jewish thing than a God thing. O my God, there is something here. You are real, we are real, this is a holy world. What can we do with it? How can we help? Does caring have a place? I know I am destructive. And like the Alcoholics Anonymous person, I want help, I want help. And I want to help the other person.

All that is part of the emotional muscles we are missing. We have to grow enough to struggle with our rage, our destructive self. To say, this is not what I want to be. Something else is there that wants to come out.

VJD: You've given your life to working within a psychoanalytic tradition while still articulating a vision of transformation…one unlike anyone else I've read or heard. Do you have hope?

ME: With individuals, yes! As far as the larger scene—national, global, institutional—I don't have that perspective. I would like to think that individuals do make a difference. If we keep working with our beings, ourselves...

I often get letters from people saying things like, "When I read you I hear my voice." Something deeper, personal, necessary comes through. Writing is part of my life and is a life and death matter. It expresses realities that seek a hearing. We each contribute what is ours to contribute, a dance, a song, a look, a touch. Help comes from everywhere; we are very sensitive beings. Cruelty and caring are twins that challenge us. We are multi-headed, multi-souled. When someone lets me know, "I hear myself in your words," I thank God for spots of connection, moments of communication, when one soul means something to another.

But I don't have any illusions about change. I don't know how to make change happen, or to change myself. No tricks. Just keep working, finding, feeling, thinking, communicating, just keep at it. I don't know much about making change. I hear about change makers taking charge. I doubt that's what I can do. Maybe I try to monkey around a bit in the basement. [We both laugh.]

I enjoy this work with the waters that flow through the psyche, the flow that is the psyche. Psychic respiration, circulation, digestion—it's a mysterious process, how one person affects another. Quality of attunement is only a start. It's a treacherous business. Lives depend on it. But it is worth the try.

VJD: And in your most hopeful scenario for the future?

ME: Jesus said the poor will always be with us. Let's hope he meant the modest and the humble aspects of the psyche. We can work on the chaff and not let the fact that bad things are happening keep us from helping. Things look pretty bleak one moment, but no one moment is all of history. Rivers get polluted and over time cleanse themselves. Sometimes it's better to adopt a long-range view. Things move this way, that way. No one slide is final.

It's part of the paradox of living that keeping the long view in mind enables one to be in the here and now. Water finds its way around barriers. There is more for a life to look after than any life can exhaust. It's not necessary to make believe things are better than they are in order to give yourself fully to the plenty you can do. Is it true that a thing of beauty is a joy forever? If so, how? I'm a hopeless romanticist because I really do feel hopeful, that there is a way to keep life fresh and open right up to, and through, the end.

1   D.T. Suzuki, *Mysticism: Christian and Buddhist: The Eastern and Western Way* (New York: Routledge, 2002, 1975).

Rodney Smith
Living and Dying without Pretension

"We can't be anything but a real human being when we die. Dying won't allow any pretension."

"Dying makes life immediately real."

"The possibility for a good death is always there. Whether I am up to the task isn't really the point. Death always holds the possibility of growth."

S OMETIMES LIFE GIVES US a gift. Sometimes at crucial moments in our lives we are presented with new paths, opportunities to grow in ways we never expected. If we have courage to take these new directions, we expand, becoming more than we ever dreamed we might become, discovering ways to live and to die with dignity and grace. That is the story of Rodney Smith's life journey as he told it to me one sunny December day in Seattle. This is how he came to work in hospice care for the last two decades, how he came to write *Lessons from the Dying* (1998), and finally, how he came to begin to "live the question of life" in each moment, in every new day as a Buddhist practitioner and teacher.

Rodney Smith was raised in Ohio. He was drafted during the Vietnam War and worked in a hospital in Belgium. On returning to Ohio, he considered going to medical school before settling on social work. His work came easily, but increasingly he felt "an inner restlessness of spirit." A spiritual direction suddenly opened when he went to hear Ram Dass speak in Cincinnati one cold spring evening. In 1979 he met Burmese monk, Mahasi

Sayadaw. Inspired, he moved to Burma and became a monk. Later he moved to Thailand for further practice. After four years he returned to the U.S seeking more social engagement. "Seeking silence," he said, "I could avoid the abrasive quality of other people until I realized that I needed to move towards what was difficult. I didn't know what I needed to learn but I knew it would be with other people." For sixteen years he worked in hospice settings in Texas, Massachusetts, and Seattle. Half of that time has been delivering direct service to those at the end of life; the other half has been as administrator and teacher of hospice staff. Today he works as the founder and guiding teacher of the Seattle Insight Meditation Society, a consultant to hospice programs, and a meditation teacher.

~

Victoria Jean Dimidjian: Death is such a central issue for you, in both your Buddhist practice and your hospice work. How is that?

Rodney Smith: Death is still a mystery. The more I work with the dying, the more life contains that mystery as well. I got involved with the dying because dying makes me come alive. Working with the dying forces me to ask questions and search for conscious ways to live.

VJD: That sounds like Buddhism.

RS: Exactly! They are two separate arenas of my life, but in many ways they are the same. Working in my first hospice I felt like I'd never left the monastery. The hospice staff didn't know a thing about Buddhism, but I could see we were facing the same fears that meditation brings forth. If I could stand the heat, I knew that the fires of death and dying could reveal eternal truths. At the monastery, my mind had been sharpened and I had learned to move towards the difficult, and now I had the subject—death and dying—to focus my mind. And death and dying began to reveal its secrets, never so we know what it is, but reveal how we fear life. So now I had to explore all the ways I was holding back from life and restricting the way I lived by distorting my life around fears of death and loss."

VJD: Is that fear gone?

RS: I must say that after all these years of hospice care, the subject of death and dying still remains as much a mystery to me now as it did then, in those first months of facing the subject. But that's the point, isn't it? That it defies an explanation, it defies a determinant sentence. It allows the continuing questioning, the ever-open question of what is the unknown and what is it like to grow old and die? What is it like to age?

VJD: So you are still afraid but you live it consciously?

RS: [He nods emphatically.] You live it consciously; you live it actively; you live the open question of death. We access the true spirit of Buddhism by living the question of life.

VJD: Let's explore that further. What do you think allowed you to stop holding back? Was it working with the dying or working with the thought of your own dying or both?

RS: Absolutely both! This is really an important point. When you start getting involved with Buddhism, you start to work on what constrains your consciousness. And what is it but fear? When you start to explore fear, inevitably it is going to lead you to death, dying, aging and all of that. So when I came back from my "Buddhist years" in the East, I wasn't going to follow social norms and not talk about death. I found people and settings where I felt comfortable to talk about these taboo subjects. That is the real spirit of the Sangha, of community. It is a place to go outside the social norms and discuss what really matters to you.

VJD: Did you have that in Texas?

RS: No, not in general, but I had it with the staff of the hospice. The hospice staff don't know Buddhist terms but they can look at death and dying and the unknown. And when you orient yourself to an unknown, you orient yourself to Buddhism. In hospice care, you have to learn to let go if you are going to survive more than a few months. Being in the place of letting go allows a kind of mystery to unfold. All the defenses we usually put in front of that mystery—to protect ourselves, to keep it safe and secure—all that goes. Hospice staff have to relish the unknown to continue to do this work, to be able to work with dying every day. The worlds of Buddhism and hospice care fit together nicely for that very reason.

VJD: Have you seen changes in the integration of Eastern spirituality in the West, not just in work with the dying but in all the human sciences?

RS: Yes. [He nods deeply and sets aside his empty tea cup.] I think the East offers ways to hold one's inward life and a way to relate to people who are in pain. These are strategies that we miss in our Western psychology and social work. If I'm angry, it doesn't mean I have to revolt against my anger or think I'm a bad person. Rather that anger—or fear or impatience or loneliness or neediness—whatever the difficult emotions that might arise—has a purpose. Typically the West doesn't give them that legitimacy. I like to frame it in terms of our aliveness. All parts of our consciousness are parts of what it means to be alive. To be fully alive means we honor and allow all aspects of our consciousness to live without internal judgment. We live as an open field, not a closed container. We can then learn to hold our inward life, not live at its expense.

VJD: Are you referring to how we censor or deny our thoughts and feelings?

RS: Censoring has the effect of limiting our ability to listen internally. Where we censor we cannot heal. Only through listening can we offer the healing qualities of awareness, attention, and mindfulness without reactivity. Through awareness, I can create the same safe environment for others that I created inside for myself. You are not going to feel safe if I ridicule or inhibit your natural expression of life…or even if I flinch! If I give any little indications that what you are expressing is off the mark, you aren't safe. But if I can create a space that allows you to be without my aversion or annoyance or disapproval, this is the environment of acceptance.

We haven't really learned to do this because we haven't learned to hold our own pain. I had a beautiful example of that in my hospice work. I was working with a woman whose husband was dying. I had seen her for a number of sessions. One day I came to sit with her and took the same posture I'd always assumed with her, with my hands on my knees, bending forward. She said, "You know, when you sit like that"—and she pointed at my knees—"you force me to grieve. And today I'm not ready to grieve. Today I'm angry as hell that he's dying. Are you going to be with me there too?"

VJD: We have so many prohibitions against anger and saying what is true. We don't tell people what we need. We don't confront them. Tell me more about that.

RS: The cultural niceties can't withstand the force and momentum of the death. Death just clears the table. We can't be anything but a real human being when we die. Dying won't allow any pretension. So if you look clearly at the moment of birth and then you look at the moment of death, you see the real human spirit. In between we just cover it up with pretension. When people are able to be honest, they recover themselves.

And that's love. That's compassion. The moment when you are able to hold the pain of another person without an aversive response. When I am connecting to your grief without any barriers, then true compassion can arise. It is always immediately available, but we are more focused on resisting what is happening. Resistance keeps individuality very well defined, but it does so at the sake of a greater aliveness.

VJD: Hearing you say this, I think about teaching adults to work with children. You are describing what happens when adults aren't in touch with the two-year-old inside so can't start to relate to the child crying at the door.

RS: Over a lifetime we have painted the raw wood of our true nature over and over again—layers upon layers. Spiritual practice is just stripping the wood back to its original purity. We usually take one layer off at a time because we are afraid of revealing too much. That's the reason the practice is hard. Because when you remove a layer of paint, the reasons that you put the paint on in the first place are again exposed—all the pain connected with that time in your life is revealed.

VJD: What is that process like?

RS: As we begin to do this work, we find ourselves re-experiencing those memories and fears that have defended us against pain, and so when we experience those fears, we know we are headed in the right direction. At the end of life, all our history is going to arise. It's a universal truth. There's no way you can block it. No paint can stand up to it. It's an absolute. I love absolutes because they allow no pretension. When there is nothing between a human being and his or her death, there is a natural quality to the way he or she dies. You see a few people approach their death with an understanding that eluded them in life.

VJD: It surprises me how much struggle and pain there can be associated with dying. Especially when I've read stories of the deaths of Buddhist masters. I think, "Well, they should know how to do it!"

RS: Yes, we say, "Well, somebody who has practiced meditation, that person must know how to die." But somebody who has practiced meditation does not know how to die. They know how to live in the raw quality of their humanness. Who knows what the dying process will be like?

There's a Zen story of the student coming to the Roshi who has cancer and saying, "When you begin to die, how are you going to hold the Dharma?" And the Roshi started rolling on the floor and yelling in pain. Then he got back up, sat straight and looked the student in the eye to see if he understood. There wasn't any way, you see. Everything else we bring to our death is just sophistication."

VJD: You have practiced meditation for most of your adult life. What is your practice like now, how is it part of who you are?

RS: It's more free-form now. For many years I did rigorous sitting every day and yearly retreats, and that practice was central to who I was. My practice defined me. But in the past decade my practice has changed. I still am dedicated to growing in awareness, and that is central in my life. But the line between meditation and living has been erased. I find as resistances come up I've learned not to avoid them or to act them out. Now I can follow the pain to investigate where it is that I am holding back, where I am avoiding what actually is.

My practice now is deeply me. It is an ever-increasing sensitivity to what

I am resisting in life, in the very moment of living. Pain wakes me up from my tendency to slumber. Once all the hard places are opened up, then awareness flows.

VJD: Would you have gotten to that place of understanding and acceptance without meditation?

RS: Speaking for me personally, I think not. I'm sure of that. But that's not true for everyone. Each person has an individual readiness to awaken. Some are just more ready for it than others. Some people like me just have more penance to do!

VJD: And now the door is continually open?

RS: There will be more pain and resistance, I know that about myself. Meeting death every day is my way of working on the resistance. Now the work is to remain open and move deeper into my heart through service to others.

VJD: And how do you do that? Is there a way you use to accomplish that each time?

RS: Surely not by applying a formula. And yet, there is a way of being with someone else, being wholly present and responding spontaneously as needed in the moment that feels authentic. There is a knowing when you are there.

VJD: Did that just evolve for you? If not, how did it happen?

RS: It was my hospice work and my meditation practice. I found how to meet each person's needs in the moment by being in the moment myself. There is only one way to be creative and that is to let go.

For example, I had a patient, Jack, who was dying of lung cancer. He was always short of breath and just terrified of the death facing him soon. Jack believed very literally in the Bible, and he felt he could not be afraid of dying because that denied the "living word of the book" that was central to his life. But I could see how filled with fear he was, how he was denying

God by denying the fear that took hold every time he got short of breath. So I just asked him, "So it's God's will that you are going to die?" And he agreed. Then I said, "So it seems that it's also his will that you are alive now." He agreed again. So I suggested that if he noticed his breath then he would in fact be noticing God's intention for him to live. As he began to notice his breath, he could no longer deny the fear that arose with his dying. He began to work with his pain rather than deny its existence. We were not talking about spirituality and faith in some abstract way, but working directly with his suffering here and now.

VJD: So his need to control through denial was eased?

RS: Yes, he began to face what stood in the way between his religion and his death. You can't die a scriptural death. Dying makes life immediately real.

VJD: Your words remind me again of how we often care for children, trying to control so much of their development, sometimes forcing growth rather than facilitating it.

RS: Yes, control breaks down during dying. And if there's been a strong need to control in your character, the pattern of trying to control your death will be there. And when you come to the end of what you can control there is often panic. Real panic. It's not too small a word. For many people the loss of control is the loss of who they are. Sometimes it is easier for people who have lived on the fringes of life because their lives have been out of their control. But for people of affluence and influence, prestige and status, they have usually had that sense of being in control. So the difficult conditions that life gave us while we were alive can often work towards our advantage when we are dying.

When you no longer can use your body in familiar ways or meet your own bodily needs, you are on the edge of being out of control. We become helpless like a little child again. That's a very tender edge. But even within this helplessness the person can still feel like a whole human being. You can still access the fact that you are complete. That sense of completeness can follow us, even if our bodies lose functionality. Losing everything except the essence of who we are is an available lesson at the end of life.

Everything moves away from us, our abilities, decision making, relationships, everything, except a wholeness of consciousness. If we can actually access that sense of completion, then we access a greater integrity than just the outside trappings of power and control that have covered over our wholeness from the beginning.

VJD: How do we, as caregivers, assist people in this process?

RS: Often the people around the dying person want to keep them linked to the living. So they put up pictures of the family, of the people they are leaving, instead of spiritual figures or visions of what may come during this passage. But people who are being left behind don't have to keep pulling and tugging at the wardrobe of the one dying. They can start finding ways to facilitate the passage. We can create an environment through music, through beauty, through going up to the loved one and saying, "You know, it's going to be hard for me, but it's going to be OK. I will work it out without you. I want you to have the best journey possible." This allows the dying to let go of things they haven't done and the issues they haven't resolved and move into the next dimension.

Everything that has defined us is falling apart. Everything is being taken away. We feel like everything we are is eliminated when death becomes real. And what does that mean? Ultimately it puts us into free fall. Not even being out of control! You're just in free fall, you have nothing to land on.

That's when the sense of self-preservation, the first stage of facing our death, begins. We come to death, we talk about it, we start to face it, and then we get scared. With the overwhelming sense of loss, suddenly the fear becomes real. So at first we retreat. We turn back to trying to keep control rather than moving into the unknown.

VJD: So you see definite stages in learning to accept death and to work with the dying?

RS: Yes, three at least. We struggle with our need for self-preservation. We want to learn from death but we don't really want to be touched by this monster. September 11 showed us all that so clearly. At first, we were all so overwhelmed, just broken apart by the tragedy. Our hearts opened. We knew we were all vulnerable and our hearts opened up to care and help and grief. For those first days we really were a different community, maybe a different country. But then the defenses went up and the concern for self-preservation started to divide us.

VJD: Is that when feelings of retaliation and hatred took over?

RS: Yes, when we had stopped opening to the suffering, brute force took over. Not that we didn't need to respond to the terrorism. We did; we couldn't let that keep happening. But now we have planted the seeds for more terror. During those weeks one community I work with in Canada marched as an attempt to take the time to understand what really happened rather than react. This is their banner. [He goes to the closet and pulls out a banner that reads: Never through anger does anger cease, only through understanding.]

If we can move beyond this need for self-preservation, then we come to the second stage. This stage is the comprehension of the universality of death; when I realize that everything I touch, that all of the people in my life, all of it is going to die. Whatever happens, death will finally intercede. So what is my relationship to the world, given that fact?

VJD: You are talking about impermanence...

RS: Exactly, embracing impermanence fully, accepting it totally. And then the final stage arises. The final call is toward self-exploration and understanding of the eternal. This brings us back full circle to the immediate moment, to living fully without pretense and just being.

VJD: Given what you're saying, it makes sense that all of the religious traditions view death as central.

RS: Oh yes! I think Christ was toying with our understanding when he brought the dead to life. He was saying that it's not about dying or not dying. It's about how we hold on to the world, how we live. The miracles were his attempt to show this [his sweeping gesture encompasses the whole room] is nothing really, just a play of different conditions. We lose who we really are within appearances. To see through these appearances is the final stage of our inquiry into death. Death shows us that because it takes the world away from us. In that moment it's gone, Whoosh!

That's why everybody sees the light. You take everything away—what else is there? I think in that moment we'd all see the light!

VJD: What do you think about your own death? What would a good death be for you?

RS: Ahhh, I'll have to give you two answers to that, the conventional one and the personal one.

The first answer is based mostly on my years in hospice work, and the second from meditation.

I think any situation is workable, and as long as it is workable I can be with it, learn from it. I don't need certain props or certain conditions, at least I think I don't. If I am dependent on those conditions, what happens if I have a heart attack out on the freeway? If my preconditions aren't met, is death going to be bad?

This is the issue with what we now call "a dignified death." But whether the body can care for itself or is secreting fluids all over the place, that isn't the basis of dignity. Dignity is how we hold the situation inside regardless of what is occurring. That is the sense of inward dignity that will define a good death for me. But I know there are many situations where I may not hold this kind of dignity. I may be screaming inside, I may be lost, it may be a tremendously difficult event. But the point is that the possibility for a good death is always there. Whether I am up to the task isn't really the point. Death holds the potential. Death always holds the possibility of growth.

Conventionally, a good death is seen in terms of whether you are dying in the place you want to die, most frequently the home. And whether the people you want around you are there or not. The hospice movement is the driving force for the establishment of that conventional definition of a good death. It holds a lot of merit. It's where people are most relaxed, where they feel most in control. And this is very important when people feel they are losing control in relation to everything else. But to be honest, we can create the environment but then old family patterns can come back in and, from a hospice point of view, not too many families rise to the challenge of this situation. Mostly it's complaining and bickering, the old family dynamics. So families die in character too, just as Elisabeth Kubler-Ross said people do.

VJD: So it seems you want to go beyond the idea of a good or a bad death. So that whether death is in a hospice or on the freeway, you will be able to be open to the situation when the time comes.

RS: That is my definition of a good death.

VJD: It seems very rooted in Buddhism.

RS: Central to the practice, yes. But I do think that the establishment of a conventional definition of "a good death" is very important. Dialoguing about what is a good death is a cultural movement towards greater sensitivity of heart and the beginning of the end of denial of death. I think the creation of the framework of a good death—environment, medication, financing, all of it—is very important in bringing the whole culture to the recognition of the potential of that event.

VJD: Yes, otherwise your words could be interpreted to mean that death can come however, whenever, and we just need to be ready.

RS: Some could say there's no need for hospices, no reason to fund support for the dying, so then nobody does anything. That takes us backward, and leaves us with nothing. So, you see, hospice supports the capacity for my individual definition of the good death. I could live without it if I had to, but I hope everyone has a chance to experience their good death.

VJD: Rodney, your experiences working in hospice have convinced you of its importance. What would you say to someone just starting to think about this decision? Why hospice rather than institutional care or just staying at home with family?

RS: At least four reasons come to mind!

First, patients can relax during their final journey in the place they find most familiar, their home environment. Most would readily choose this except they have no experience and knowledge to handle the physical and medical problems that emerge at the end of life. So they go to institutional settings where they think such problems can be handled. But of course hospice provides the resources to die at home. Hospice says to the patient, "You can die where you are most comfortable and with the people you are most comfortable with, and we can be there to manage the symptoms and solve the medical/physical problems during this passage."

Second, hospice looks at the patient and family as a unit of care during the terminal illness. Few institutions provide that range of support. Usually dying is seen as an individual problem, and the medical focus is on alleviating symptoms and pain for the patient. In hospice a holistic approach is used with all the family. Both patient and family members are engaged, and their psychosocial, spiritual and physical needs are supported during the transition. And then after the patient's death, support during the grieving period is given, usually for at least thirteen months for family members so bereavement can unfold naturally. Sometimes it does take longer, but usually there is some movement toward the acceptance of the death during that first year.

Third, hospice provides resources to families in their homes to make end-of-life affordable in the way they want, not having to deplete family finances to care for their dying member. Hospice has the unique knowledge and skill to train and support the family during each step of the dying process.

But, you know, I think the fourth reason is the most important thing hospice can do, and the reason I would turn to it during my dying. Hospice help is available to the patient and family at any time, day or night, just a phone call away. It's very different from having to schedule an "emergency admission" or get a doctor through the answering service. Hospice staff have immediate experience and responsive help right there. They say, "We've been through this before, we know how to work with the end of life, and here is what we can help with right now." Since this is their only focus of care, they have truly learned how to listen, how to make their specific expertise of help in the immediate moment.

VJD: So the hospice approach is a constantly-open-door link to the family and its dying member?

RS: Yes, one which makes talking about dying and expressing the struggles that are part of the process possible. Too often the dying are silenced, and their concerns and questions are inhibited, even prohibited. You know, the idea that doctors know best and the hospital will take care of everything. That kind of mentality pervades our health care delivery. But terminal illness and dying really are different, and hospice care takes a radically different stance with each. Hospice works in partnership with the family and patient, helping with each step, responding to each struggle.

VJD: What keeps you doing this work?

RS: Dealing with the rubs of life is dealing with the self. And therefore there is the ongoing work with the mystery and the unknown. Ultimately that allows us to work with our death. This is the call of spiritual growth. It need not wait until we have metastatic cancer with weeks to live. This is the call of immediacy.

VJD: So all of those things—what you call the little rubs of life to the end of life—all these things can be ways to learn to be with yourself?

RS: Exactly. Death gives us the lessons for living. It gives us the materials for meeting each moment fully and openly. When we keep our death close, we remain in touch with how to live. With death, we have no more time to procrastinate. No more endless tomorrows. Time comes screeching to a halt, and suddenly the heart opens. Why does the heart open when time isn't there? Thinking in terms of time, living in terms of time is the very blockage of the heart. How often do you say, "Oh, I can do that tomorrow" and it never gets done. We carry all the yesterdays we carry with us, all our expectations, our plans, and all that prohibits us from being fully engaged here and now. Death gives us hope. Death gives us the opportunity to live life, every moment of it, knowing life and death are one if only we can get out of the way. Opening the heart, engaging in living, that is the way of living and dying.

Sister Chân Không
Embodying the Paradox

"Right now, you are something very wonderful. But when you leave this body, you continue to be something very wonderful."

"A young tree growing is beautiful, but an old tree of seventy or eighty years is much more beautiful. It has such a story from all its years."

I INTERVIEWED Sister Chân Không on a hot July afternoon in Plum Village, France at the Buddhist retreat center where she lives. Our time together on that sun-filled afternoon flowed full of the stories, bits of songs, memories and hopes of this determined community leader, activist and Dharma teacher. The afternoon together passed so quickly, I was surprised when, after what seemed like just a short time, the dinner bell rang!

Sister Chân Không was born Cao Ngoc Phuong in Vietnam. She was ordained as a nun by Thich Nhat Hanh in 1988. From him she received the name Chân Không, "True Emptiness." Her life has been a bridge between the worlds of East and West, and activism and contemplation. Her early work focused on caring for poor people in Vietnam during the war, and later on she worked to help Vietnamese refugees and orphans. While she continues this work, she also plays a key role in providing emotional support and guidance for the monks and nuns of Plum Village. She is the author of *Learning True Love: How I Learned and Practiced Social Change in Vietnam* (Parallax Press, 1993). Her life story is an amazing balance of active caring for others and deep internal commitment to Buddhism.

༄

Victoria Jean Dimidjian: Sister, seeing the streams of people coming into Plum Village over the past days has amazed me. You and others here have such a task bringing all this together! Can you tell me more about how you do it?

Sr. Chân Không: We have so many people coming to Plum Village now! Some come by bus, by car, or sometimes people walk here. I think people come because they feel so at home here. They can be Jewish, Christian, or not religious at all. We have had many people who say when they first come here that they hate monastics because their family forced them to go to a religious school and they hated it.

VJD: So they rebelled against their tradition?

SCK: Yes, and against all spiritual traditions. They sometimes say that every time they see a monastic, they feel resentment. But after staying here they feel transformed. What was hatred of the monastic way is changed. That is the living, engaged spiritual tradition we want to offer here. Every day we offer material food and spiritual food. In the past, perhaps people had to go to church one day of the week, but this isolates spirituality from living. Here, we want to offer a living spirituality.

VJD: Let's begin with how you came to Buddhism and how Buddhism became part of your life as you journeyed from East to West.

SCK: I was born in Vietnam in 1938 during the war time. My family was not poor but not rich either. Even when I was so young, I wondered why there were so many hungry children. I saw poor families that worked hard and had nothing to eat. I didn't have to work that hard and my parents fed me.

VJD: So you were already aware of other's suffering...

SCK: Yes, and of my parent's generosity, too. My mother always had a little savings and she would let people borrow from her to set up businesses. Sometimes these businesses—street vendors selling breakfasts, businesses like that—were successful and they would pay my mother back and become like part of the family. And sometimes their businesses would fail and that was okay too in my family—they would still be considered part of the family. So I had both experiences, of witnessing suffering and witnessing generosity.

When I was thirteen I left my home family to go to Saigon to go to high school in the city. I went to school in the mornings, then home for lunch and right away did my homework. When I was done I looked around to see what I could do to help the families in the slum areas with no food, the children with no school to go to. I went with a rice bag to each family in the area where we lived and asked each family to put one handful in the bag each time they cooked rice. You know, rice in Vietnam is like bread here.

So with each meal, each family put aside one handful in the bag. Soon every house had a bag of rice ready for me. I came every month and brought the bags to the slum children who had no school at all to give them a "scholarship of rice." So that each child would have food every day. I invited my friends in school and my younger sister to do this work and they all joined in. It was so joyful.

We also helped them go to school. They told me the school said they had no birth certificates so they could not come to school. I inquired at the school and at the police, and I found out how to get the certificates. I got the papers and helped them to write all the information, then we sent it to the tribunal. We all helped with this. And then they each had a birth certificate. And the work went on very beautifully. We were helping many families, many children.

VJD: So your first work of helping children came before you began practicing Buddhism?

SCK: In those days in South Vietnam there was already Buddhism of course. But much of it was just reciting the sutras. It was just a tradition of chanting priests. They chanted at funerals, but they didn't know the teaching of the Buddha. These so-called priests ignored the needs of the people.

Of course some of the Buddhist leaders did more. They were engaged in helping the poor and they were imprisoned. The authorities thought they were part of the revolution so they were sent away to some remote place.

VJD: That seems true in Western religions as well, that they are too often only practiced at birth and at death, not for all the time we are living.

SCK: Yes, we all have the problem of making a religious practice that is engaged and connected to lives and human needs.

VJD: What inspired you to help those children?

SCK: The reason came from inside me, from seeing there was something unfair and something I must do to help. It was after this that my family decided that I should go back to the home province to take the five precepts of Buddhism. There was a big teacher coming from Saigon and I went back for the summer holidays and listened to his talk. But I had so many questions! And I didn't feel satisfied with his answers. Afterwards the monk said I should ask this other monk who was there with him, a man who looked very humble but had answers that were very profound. I was very impressed. The answers satisfied all my rational way of thinking and arguing and wanting always to know why, and then I wanted to become a Buddhist. But the monk said I should take my time to learn. My mind should find the answers.

I am a very passionate person and after that I went every place there was a Buddhist teacher giving a Dharma talk. I went to talks in the city and out in the countryside. And at every talk I gave a critique, "Oh, this one is very good" or "Oh, this one is OK." The more I learned of Buddhism, the more I thought the Buddha was a great person. Even though he could have become a king, instead he worked only to help people. I asked why there were so many poor people and no Buddhist institutions to help the orphans and the poor children and the elderly. And my first teacher, Thich Thanh Tu, said that the aim of Buddhism is to help people to understand that you take care of each other and that a family shares what it can share. It may not be much but that's OK.

At that time, I visited one of the older Catholic orphanages and saw 100 children in the care of just one sister. Oh, and it was so poor, and run just like an army, bang, bang! I was shocked. The children needed love. So I organized my friends so that we could be big sisters for four girls and big brothers for four boys. We would try to visit every week, bringing candies and playing sports and getting permission to take them to the zoo or the botanical garden. This is how I practiced Buddhism this way until I met with Thầy [Thich Nhat Hanh].

When I graduated from high school, I began studying at the university in Saigon. Whenever I asked very difficult questions, someone would take a book by Thầy and say, "If you read that book, you will know." But I was a very active person! I didn't want to sit down and read. Then one Sunday, I went to hear Thầy and I was so impressed. What I liked about Thầy's teaching was that when I asked a question and I expected an answer like my former teacher always gave me, he would only listen, listen and smile. Now at retreats on the last day he will always answer at the question and answer time, but then he would never answer my questions. Maybe he could read my mind. He knew I wanted to have an answer in order to go and argue with my friends. At that time intellectual curiosity at the university was of highest importance. And we would argue, all of us, Catholics, Buddhists, teachers. But not Thầy. It was later on that I learned that it was not true Buddhism to get the answer but to live the answer in your practice. Thầy didn't want to transform me into a lawyer for Buddhism. He wanted me to practice and to share from the inside love.

VJD: Not from words or argument—

SCK: Yes! I came to understand that! Slowly I became more and more vegetarian. If we eat less meat, we are more respectful to life. And also if you cannot even kill a chicken, then when you are angry at someone you really cannot do harm to that person. This teaching is not non-action but the practice of mindful action of compassion. I have to look deep, to go to those parts of myself and then put what I understand into practice. So this is truly engaged Buddhism. In the past perhaps I did good work. But now the teaching of the Buddha affects every part of my life, how I walk and what I eat and what I do—

VJD: So engagement in every moment, every day?

SCK: Yes, with your heart, your behavior, your way of looking and act-ing and speaking. Since I met Thây when we were so very young—it was 1959—he already embodied the practice of non-form, the most essential teaching of Buddhism. And even in those days he read the Bible, and he found so many good things that my Christian friends never said. He saw that the beauty is deep, is everywhere. He read out Islam, the Koran and he found that beauty everywhere. In Buddhism you are free to read all, and if you find beauty there, you are free to share.

VJD: What led you to become a nun?

SCK: My first teacher had said if I wanted to become enlightened, I must become a nun. So I visited many nuns, stayed with them, heard them chanting, but I was not inspired. I did not see joy in their practice. I did not want to live like that. Later, Thây said, "What you have done is great because we have to manifest compassion into action." He helped me see that the teaching of the Buddha is real social change, helping people to stand up and light their own torches and find a new way.

This was in the time the country was at war, and communism was urg-ing all the poor people to fight against the rich who had exploited them, creating anger and hatred and more suffering. What I wanted was social change that would come from the heart, not from outside but from within. Thây said we should go to the countryside and stay with the poor. I went back and started a school with seventy-seven children. We studied just under the trees or, if it rained, on the veranda of a house.

We had a new notion of Buddhism. Before, we went to the temple and there were chants and we earned some merit painting the temple and serv-ing the Buddha, but what the Buddha truly needs is for us not to serve the temple but the children in need. Soon one person said he had palm leaves to give, and another bamboo, and in a few weeks we had built a school. The revolution came from our work. We tried to practice at every step, and we had one week each month for mindfulness.

VJD: Do you maintain this mixture of spirituality and external work in your daily life now?

SCK: Here in Plum Village we are now more than 200 brothers and sisters, but we always train ourselves to live like a family, a big family! If people from such different places can practice to love their brothers and sisters, then it will be possible to love everyone. You learn to love people in other families, to love all. Building a relationship is like growing a tree. You start with the seed and have to cultivate it until it becomes strong. You have to appreciate it every day, every week, not just when there is some problem. And if there is a hurt, you don't speak right away. It doesn't mean that you bury the hurt! But that inside you calm down. You wait a few days, and then you speak about what you appreciate about that person, you tell them that before you tell them about the hurt you have. You do not judge. You talk to explore the reasons. No condemnation, just expression in an open way.

VJD: So the relationship then can start to change?

SCK: Yes, the Buddha preached impermanence, that everything is change. A mother came to talk with me about her son. He was a musician and he refused to see her. I don't know, maybe she had hurt him so much. And now she was so hurt. So I proposed that she go to his concerts like an admirer, even though he never returned her calls or her letters. Before going, she should call and leave a message on the machine expressing her admiration of his work, sowing the seeds of her appreciation. Not bringing up the divorce when he was young and how she gave everything for him, not having any expectations. And she went. After the concert, she wrote her son one letter each week expressing her appreciation. Slowly, the relationship began to change. Now, after many years, she and her son and her grandson are a family again.

VJD: Sister, in the West most of us are very afraid to think about death. In fact, we fear it deeply and avoid facing the inevitability of dying. It seems to me there is a different way in the East and a different understanding in Buddhism. How is it for you as you age?

SCK: Imagine that you are coming to a new house. You come into the courtyard and see all the beautiful plants and benches and trees. Then you come to the lovely door and you enter the house. And when you are far inside, you see the true treasure. Coming into Buddhism is like coming to the treasure. At first, you are excited about the sitting meditations. This keeps you quiet, at peace inside, and you think this is enough. But in Buddhism the most profound teaching is about death. And we are all going to die.

We are each like a cloud in the sky. The cloud knows he is going to die. He could be so fearful! But when the cloud ceases to be a cloud, when the cold air comes, he will become snow. The snow is wonderful, each piece like a little cloud. Then the snow becomes water, and this water makes the grass very green. So you begin to see that you cannot die. One day your heart ceases to beat. Right now, you are something very wonderful. But when you leave this body, you continue to be something very wonderful. Just as you sit in this room with me now, very peaceful. And then you step out of the room and you close the door, now are you peaceful? When you step out of this body, are you still peaceful? You can continue to be.

Sometimes I imagine I am on an airplane and someone tells me there is hijacker and the plane will explode. What will I do? I will say, "I am a cloud, I am changing like the cloud. Now I will be space, free. When it explodes I will be melted and I am not afraid."

Before you die you have time to become a cloud. One day, one week, one year, you can do this. If you live fully in the present moment. There are people who live thirty years in forgetfulness. If you can look deeply into the nature of things—into a flower or a cloud—you will be so peaceful. Yes, one day you will feel tired and old, then you may die. But like the flower, another life will grow and become beautiful.

Sometimes we have people coming here who are ill and they want to learn to die. But, instead, they learn how to live in the present moment. One man came who was in chemotherapy for a long time. He came just before his last chemotherapy session. And he was weak, but he came to listen. I said, "Maybe your ears are weak now, but there are hundreds of people here with earphones on who are continuing to share the Dharma." He stayed here for one month. When he died, his wife was very sad. She grieved for him and missed him very much. Even though his form was not here, he was present in his children, in his grandchildren, in all he had made. He was an artist, and the family remembered all his work, remembered every word he has said. So he was present with them still. Because you do not see your husband does not mean that he is not still in his children, his friends, in you.

Of course, that doesn't mean that when I hear that I have cancer and will die tomorrow I will be very happy. When I found out I had some cancerous growth, I felt so sad. But I practiced deep relaxation and sitting every day. I thought I had a tumor. But I sat and thought if I am not to be in this form, then I will be in another form. So I started to look at the new monastics, trying in a skillful way to prepare for my passing away. Finally, the doctors told me it was not cancer. Not normal either, a tumor, but not cancer. They removed the tumor and said to come back in three months, and then they kept watch. And now twenty years have passed—

VJD: Twenty years, oh!

SCK: For me that tumor was like a day of mindfulness, reminding me to be more careful about my health and how I live. This practice is to teach touching happiness, so I tried to advise people as I do myself, to be mindful and to stay in touch with what is wonderful. At any age you can be young, that is your spirit. One sister made a cake, and I said, "Oh, this is like the cake of my childhood!" So we took some and tasted like a little child does. At every age you can be joyful. When you are young, you have that simple joy of being young. But when you are old, still be joyful.

There is nothing to be fearful about being old. When you are forty years old, you are beautiful with freshness but not much maturity. At fifty you still have some freshness but your skin is much less smooth than at twenty years. At seventy years old, your health is less good than fifty but that is okay. Each age has its beauty. A young tree growing is beautiful, but an old tree of seventy or eighty years is much more beautiful. It has such a story from all its years.

I had a grandnephew who died very young. And his father, my nephew, told me that all the good qualities of his son now entered his younger brother who became so kind, and so caring. The boy who died was very loving and generous. The hospital asked if the family would give his kidneys and liver for other children, and my nephew said yes. But afterwards he said, "How could I give the body of my son to others?" I think the boy's spirit helped him to say yes and give this. One year before I was born, my mother miscarried a boy. Maybe at the moment a year ago my mother had conceived me, but my heart was not very good and I didn't want to appear with a weak heart. So I withdrew and then appeared again.

In Buddhism we think we are not one, not separate, not different. That little boy is you, and at twenty he is also you. And you are not the same, but you are not different. Of course there is abrupt birth and death, but this is taking new forms. According to the teaching of Buddha, there is no separate self. So you can be reborn in another son, another friend. You are not different, not the same but not different. So I am sure that when I know I am going to die, I will be shocked. But not too long. Those who do not know the profound teaching of the Buddha suffer this pain all their lives. But for me, I think the shock will be short and then I will go on.

VJD: So dying is still a way to practice, still a way to know...

SCK: Yes, yes. A way to make life beautiful even if you are in the worst situation. If you have a spiritual life, instead of complaining about your fate, you know what to do to make life wonderful. Even if you are paralyzed, you can move your hand. Or if you cannot move your hand, you can open your mouth to say something. If not that, you blink your eyes to communicate something.

My mother passed away in a very happy way. I could not visit her every day since I lived in Plum Village. I invited her to come here but she didn't feel comfortable with the monastics, so she stayed with her daughter and with her son. And every time I called her, I made her very happy. For her birthday, instead of sending a cake, I wrote the story of how she met my father, putting in all the wonderful things. I try to help my nephew, niece, brother and sister as they care for her. And I see her continuation in each of them. She had nine children, and all her children share with poor people like she did. I said to her, "Mom, you don't have only one heart. You have nine more hearts! And then you have the continuation, now sixty-four wonderful hearts to share, to give to poor people."

I tell her, "Mom, in the past you cooked so well. Now you cannot handle the knife to peel the carrot, but it is the same hand that cooked so well for all of us. You see, you will be forever." To me it is like the old car. Now the new car of the granddaughter is coming, and her eyes look like the eyes of my mother eighty years ago. The joy she was is now the joy of this girl. Here at Plum Village, we are trained to care. A nun accepts another's mother as her mother, the father is the father of all. Some sisters have brought their mothers or fathers here, and we try our best to create a joyful home for them here. To make life and death just a continuation of a wonderful journey, helping them to take a new form so life can continue. At my funeral I would like all to say, "Happy Continuation, Sister!" [She laughs.] This morning a sister whom I had trained sang, and I see her success at singing so beautifully as my success. If the sisters are happy and joyful and successful, then it is also my continuation.

VJD: So you will grow old at Plum Village, with joy?

SCK: With joy, with singing, with teaching the words of the Buddha. Yes, continuing each day, then coming to the quiet, to the last breath, to the time of change and forever.

John Welwood
The Story of Life and Death

"Each moment is completely fresh. This moment, this now, will never be again."

"The essential spiritual practice, whether we are young or old, is to learn to ride the wave and be at one with it, to be with what is in each moment."

"Learning how to be fully present with our experience is the best practice for dying as well as living."

JOHN WELWOOD is a clinical psychologist, writer, and Buddhist practitioner. He is the author of seven books including the best-selling *Journey of the Heart: The Path of Conscious Love* (Shambhala Publications, 1983). He is also a leading authority on East/West psychology. His writings address the dynamic and essential connection between psychotherapy and spiritual practice. Welwood was born in Massachusetts nearly sixty years ago and completed his undergraduate education at Bowdin College with a year of undergraduate study at the University of Paris. He then moved to the Midwest where he did master's and doctoral work at the University of Chicago, writing a unique dissertation that challenged traditional psychoanalytic tenets. The following year he moved to northern California where he has taught at four different universities and professional training institutes as well as conducting a private practice. In the early Eighties, he served as director of the East/West Psychology Program at the California Institute of Integral Studies in San Francisco for several years.

On a sunny September morning, I journeyed from Berkeley across the

San Rafael Bridge into Marin county where John lives. It was a time when all the news was of potential war with Iraq and life felt tenuous and strained. But driving through the hills along the coast, then gazing at two hawks swooping in the sky, every minute spoke of idyllic peace. John's welcoming smile as he ushered me into his house made it easy to begin our conversation.

~

Victoria Jean Dimidjian: So could you talk a bit first of how you came to both Buddhism and psychology, how you began to bring them together?

John Welwood: My own journey began as many of our generation were turning East. In 1963 I spent a year in Paris. I had been studying existentialism, which was quite meaningful to me, but I had also arrived at a point where the existential heroic journey to create meaning in a meaningless world felt like a dead end. Then I came across Alan Watt's *Psychotherapy East and West* in a Paris bookshop. I realized that the problem was not so much the absurdity of the world, as the distortions of the ego. That had a big impact on me.

Discovering Zen through my readings of Watts and D.T. Suzuki gave me a whole new perspective. The idea that we can discover our true nature, realize it experientially, that was revolutionary. I was also deeply influenced by Watt's idea that Western psychotherapy could be a potential force for awakening, especially for Westerners.

So I decided to go to graduate school in psychology. At the University of Chicago, I met Eugene Gendlin. When I first heard Gendlin speak about his understanding of the experiential process, I felt that I had entered a whole new world. I had never heard anyone speak about the process of experiencing before, much less as eloquently as he did. He was also doing groundbreaking work on helping people tune into their bodily felt experience and draw on that to find directions for growth and change. He helped me understand and work with the actual process of experiencing and the personality change that happens in psychotherapy. He was my first real teacher.

VJD: And were you practicing Buddhism at this time?

JW: Mostly reading and study. It was still theoretical for me then. I went to the Chicago Zen Center, but not regularly. I didn't find a Buddhist teacher until a few years later, after I'd moved to the West Coast and started my career in teaching and clinical work here. It was the Tibetan teacher Chogyam Trungpa Rinpoche who had the biggest impact on me. I'd never met such an intriguing, inscrutable, challenging, and provocative human being! You never knew what he'd do or say next. I went into a room for an interview with him once early on and felt like the space had expanded, as if the walls had just fallen away. His presence was amazing.

He was insistent that sitting on the cushion was the way. You know, I was pretty resistant to that then. It didn't make a lot of sense to me. [He laughs.] It seemed so very old-fashioned, I thought there must be some more high-tech way to go about changing consciousness. But I felt so intrigued and challenged by Trungpa Rinpoche that I finally decided to give meditation a try. How can I be an explorer of consciousness, I thought, and not find out what meditation is all about?

Meditation opened up my world in a whole new way. We have this incredible instrument, called the mind, which allows us to experience everything from heaven to hell and all that's in between. But it's given to us without any operating instructions! Meditation started to provide me with a path for working with the mind. It's remained an important pathway ever since.

VJD: Do you have a teacher today?

JW: I currently study with a Dzogchen teacher, Tsognyi Rinpoche.

VJD: You've been linking psychology and Buddhism for nearly thirty years. Where are you now in your work?

JW: Psychological work is a process of unfolding, a process of opening up your experience and finding out what is there, hidden or implicit within it. It's like unpacking a suitcase that was packed a long time ago, and you've forgotten what's in there. You're surprised to find what's there, even though when you find it, there's a sense of recognition. Aha! This process of unfolding happens sequentially, in time, through a stepwise process of inquiry, where you pose certain questions and feel into your bodily-sensed knowing to let answers emerge. I call this "horizontal work" because the discovery is a gradual, evolving process of unfolding that happens in steps.

Meditative practice—or any deep spiritual work—is more "vertical" in that it involves cutting through the stuff of the mind and moving into radically deeper states of presence, right on the spot, instead of trying to explore or understand particular experiences. Meditation practice is training in looking into your present experience, not to unpack it or resolve your issues, but to drop all concepts so that you can be freshly in the moment.

The way I work is an integration of psychological and spiritual work in this sense: There is an unpacking, unfolding process, where we follow the experiential process very closely, but we do it in the service of developing a deeper quality of presence, making direct contact with our essential being. This is much more significant than just unpacking the bags. However, unpacking or unfolding can be a vehicle for what I call "vertical shifts"—moments when someone drops into a deeper quality of connection with who they essentially are.

Spiritual work is more about discovering who you really are and surrendering to something larger than yourself. It allows for vertical shifts that cut through to the essence of what we are—pure, non-conceptual presence and timeless awareness—which underlies everything we think, do, and experience. It is a dimension of spaciousness and depth.

VJD: You seem to be talking about a lifelong process.

JW: The process of discovery in the horizontal and vertical dimensions is endless. Uncovering the hidden truths in our life experience can eventually start dropping you to a deeper level of fully being there with yourself. The unpacking prepares the way for a deepening, so that you are more present in, with, and for yourself. And this capacity to connect with and settle into our being in the present moment is the ultimate resolution of most of our problems. When that truly happens, resolving issues is no longer the primary concern. In fact, I don't know that we ever truly resolve any issues—except insofar as they clear up on their own. But when you're able to be present in yourself, you relate to your issues in a different way. They no longer prevent you from being, being happy, being at peace. Peace and happiness only arise out of being established in our own deeper nature.

In my work, this deeper connection arises out of unpacking, understanding, seeing where something is going or where it leads. By coming into direct contact with what is really true for yourself, you develop more capacity to be with what is going on in each moment, leading to sudden openings. The shift cuts through your fixation on your particular states of mind, and you find yourself standing in a whole new place.

Trying to effect spiritual development through waging war on ourselves is always a mistake. We don't change by trying to change ourselves, or fighting with who we are. Rather, we change by coming to fully know, accept, embrace who we are.

VJD: Do you think the capacity to enter that deeper place is at all connected with the aging and the maturing process?

JW: No, I think it's ageless. It hasn't been my experience that people in later stages of life have more access to this. Anyone can experience timeless moments of pure, transparent consciousness at any time. Even children can have spontaneous mystical experiences.

One might think that it would come with maturity. But maturity is our flowering as a person who can relate to life fully. Where maturation plays a part is in our capacity to integrate spiritual realizations and practice into our daily life. That kind of integration is more likely as we grow older.

In the early years of my spiritual practice, I felt the excitement of discovery, but it was hard to fully make those discoveries part of my life. Many of us who have explored the Eastern teachings have had that struggle. In first receiving the teachings, we were just neophytes. It was like the excitement of new converts. But then it became apparent that for me and many of my fellow seekers, the spiritual journey wasn't well integrated with our lives. It didn't fully translate into how we were living, relating to each other, acting in the world. So the developmental issue is how you integrate it.

VJD: So you live it wholly, as opposed to separating the spiritual domain from the rest of one's life?

JW: Yes. For example, I often do retreats, have rich experiences, and then return with a purity or clarity of consciousness. Yet it is often hard sustain this clarity when I return home. In a culture like Tibet's, there wasn't that much of a gap between being in a cave and being in Lhasa. People walked around the city spinning their prayer wheels, after all! But in a culture like ours, which is so materialistic, pressured, confused, it's an enormous challenge to maintain a spiritual practice and spiritual life, and to integrate one's spiritual understanding into all the facets of our life.

VJD: Another challenge that our culture is facing is that of an aging population. We wonder how will we live our last years and how will we face the end of life. Have you given much thought to conscious dying and what a good death would be?

JW: I don't think about death as some special thing apart from living. Dying is happening all the time in our life. When we are attentive to the flux of life, we see nothing is lasting. Each moment ends, and a new moment arises. The person I was as a child is not who I am now. Who I was as a student in Chicago died long ago. Who I was last year has died and who I was yesterday has also died. The only thing that persists is the story in our mind that we are creating. It's the mind that maintains the sense of continuity, believing that who I am today is the same self I was yesterday.

You ask a question and even though I have written books on the subject, I don't have an answer on the tip of my tongue because what I might say right now is not the same as what I would have said yesterday or this morning. At each moment I keep having a new take on everything we're talking about. That also makes writing books challenging, because by the time I've come to the end of the book, my ideas have undergone quite a bit of alteration and refinement, forcing me to go back and rewrite from the beginning; and at the end of each draft, I have come to a different perspective yet again. This is a sign of the open-ended nature of reality. This is also why the relationship between the psychological and the spiritual remains a living question for me, because there are no final answers to it.

Something arises, it seems true for a while, and then I see a new angle that I did not see before. The old perspective has died. This is true of everything—our feelings, our beliefs, our relationships, our sense of life, and what we are doing here. We need to develop a sensitivity to impermanence. That's the basis of spiritual life. But, unfortunately, that too can become just another static concept: Impermanence, oh yeah, everything's impermanent.

VJD: And it is!

JW: Sure! But what does that really mean? It's not just that things die. It's that each moment is completely fresh. This moment, this now, will never be again. We've talked for half an hour, and the thoughts and perceptions I had a few minutes ago are already gone.

So each moment arises completely different, unique, and fresh. But our thoughts make it seem as though life is a continuity, like a movie that keeps unrolling. In truth, the movie is only made up of a sequence of separate and unique frames. William James pointed out how the mind creates the illusion of continuity. Consciousness is a stream of freshly arising moments, but it appears to be continuous, James said, because each thought grasps onto the previous thought, as in a relay race, and carries it further. This passing along of the baton makes the stream of consciousness seem continuous.

VJD: Yes, and the race is linear, too. We go from here to there.

JW: Yes. So death is the ending of the body, and of the self in this particular form, but consciousness isn't anything solid, continuous, or enduring. Recognizing that wakes us up, whereas if we think there is just one big movie going on, we tend to fall asleep in it, and fail to notice the vibrancy and open-endedness of each moment.

The challenge then is to live each moment and be awake to this moment just as it is, discovering there is nothing here to hang onto. That is a way of relating to death as an intimate part of life. Recognizing the freshness of each moment wakes us up from the dreams and movies created by the mind. Then we can look, see, touch, and feel directly. When we let go of our fixation on our thoughts, and let go of the baton that the last thought shoves into our hand, we experience a moment of both dying and coming alive at the same time.

VJD: But for many of us that seems to be harder as we age and we face death.

JW: We can wake up from the dream projections in our mind at any moment. This requires a practice of letting go of expectations of how life should be. We have all kinds of expectations about life: I shouldn't be dying. I should stay alive. I shouldn't be in pain. I should be happy. But the energy and pulse of life moves in waves with continuous ups and downs, expansion and contraction, ebb and flow. We try to cut the wave in half so that we don't have to experience the down cycle, but this cuts us off from life and makes us rigid. The essential spiritual practice, whether we are young or old, is to learn to ride the wave and be at one with it, to be with what is in each moment.

VJD: How about loss?

JW: Gain and loss are the up and down cycles of the wave. The only way to accept loss is to open to it as a bodily felt experience, and to be present with how it feels, rather than holding on to an expectation that it shouldn't be happening.

   I don't want to suggest that we should be readily able to do this. It may take a lot of work on oneself before little glimmers of that can happen. It requires coming up against our habits of denial, not wanting to be present with our experience as it is.

   Learning how to be fully present with our experience is the best practice for dying as well as living. Preparing for death involves being able to be deeply in touch with what is happening, and being able to acknowledge it as it happens. Then as the body dissolves, it's possible we could experience that directly, even open into the experience, rather than freaking out. Being able to say "yes" to what is, that's the essence of the spiritual path.

VJD: It seems also that the work of learning to be fully present in relationship with others is also the model for being fully present with death.

JW: Yes, but in all our relationships we constantly want them to be a certain way. That's the big problem, always wanting to have our partner be a certain way, to have the relationship go a certain direction, to have our children be what we want them to be. But nothing in life ever fits our image, least of all other people. And we're constantly fighting with our partner, or ourselves, or the relationship for not living up to our expectation.

And so when we're dying, we might wind up saying, "This isn't how it should be. I didn't think it would end like this!"

VJD: So perhaps all the writing about the good death, the conscious death, could be misleading?

JW: Yes, it can be. Once we formulate ideas about "the good death" we create another set of expectations to live up to. The poet Rilke wrote about the importance of everyone finding their own individual death. Learning how to be fully present with our experience is the best practice for dying as well as living. The thirteenth of the *Sonnets to Orpheus* begins,

> Be ahead of all parting, as though it already were
> Behind you, like the winter that has just gone by.
> For among these winters there is one so endlessly winter
> that only by wintering through it will your heart survive.

I have a friend who put together a CD with various teachers guiding you into the death experience, but the problem with that is that it gives people definite ideas about dying that could interfere with the individual's unique experience of death. This is one of the most important moments in life, the final passage we make. Personally, I wouldn't want to live someone else's version of that!

VJD: The good part of that is that we are living in a time now of opening things up, finding the words. Whether it's sex or birth or menopause or death—all of these things that years ago weren't talked about. But doesn't that seem like such a Western idea, to get a handle on it, a how-to-do-it process?

JW: Yes, it's good that we can talk openly about death. But the danger is that we create a model of how to go about it. Whole industries grow up around something like that! The whole point is that death is the time to let go of all your ideas and expectations.

So the danger with talking too much about death is that we try to make it something known and package the experience in familiar concepts. It's like talking about God, and imagining that we really know what we're talking about, when the reality is totally beyond all our concepts. That can prevent us from experiencing freshly, that's the danger. Talking, reading, and preparing is good up to a point. But I imagine dying is more like taking a leap, which nothing, finally, can prepare you for. If you've ever taken a psychedelic drug, for example, you may have all kinds of ideas about what will happen and how you can prepare for it, but when the experience starts happening, forget it! Forget anything you ever thought about it. The experience is so far beyond all of that!

VJD: I've spent my life in education, and educators are famous for doing that. A program for this, a curriculum for that.

JW: Exactly. Education—like death—is not about products or formulas. Dying your own death is opening to what is right as it's happening.

VJD: And the more you try to control it, the more difficult it will be.

JW: And the weirder! Because the whole experience is beyond control. It demands giving in to the experience. So the preparation is learning to be in the moment, without any "shoulds." To be ready for death, as the final part of our journey, the last unknown, comes from learning to live and be present.

VJD: You've been a leader in integrating Eastern and Western ideas as well as understanding of life psychologically and spiritually. Many others are working in this field now, too. Where do you see the field going from here? Will we in the West be able to draw more upon this?

JW: The differences between East and West are still very deep. The East emphasizes liberation from the human condition, while the Western spiritual traditions place special value on the human incarnation in its own right, and are more interested in fulfilling the meaning of this incarnation than in going beyond it or finding release from it.

At first, I was thoroughly taken with the Eastern orientation toward awakening, and it still is a central focus in my life. But these days I am more concerned with how to integrate spiritual awareness into daily life.

I've come back to my Western roots to ask: How does my understanding of things as a Westerner, which is deep in my cells and bones, fit with the Eastern view of things? Some people try to smooth over these differences in a New Age *schmear*, making them into a big smorgasbord. But I see the two traditions as very different.

One way I ask the question is: What is the relation between individuation and liberation, between becoming a person and going beyond the person altogether? I don't want to have to choose between the two. The East doesn't tell us much about individuation, and the West doesn't tell us much about liberation. To bring these two together is an important evolutionary step at this time.

Humanity discovered enlightenment thousands of years ago, and that was a tremendous discovery. But what hasn't happened yet is bringing enlightenment down to earth, having it transform life on this planet. The question is why the spiritual discoveries humanity has made have not affected how the world works, or how people get along with each other.

My sense is that developing more conscious human relationships is the next step in our evolutionary journey. Relationships between people in religious organizations and spiritual communities are no better than anywhere else, which shows us how hard it is to integrate spiritual insight into relational life. Of course, there are teachings and practices for kindness, compassion, generosity, selfless love, and service and that's wonderful. But that's still on the humanitarian level. When it comes down to on-to-one personal relationships, we're in trouble.

VJD: So you're saying we get it on the principled level, but not in actually living?

JW: As Rilke said, "For one human being to love another, this is the most difficult of all our tasks." Asia has dealt with relationships differently than we have in the West. There everyone has their set role. The mother has her role, the father his, the son knows what his role is, he relates to each parent in a specific way. It's all spelled out. Or it has been until recently. There's a set hierarchy, and everyone is plugged into their own specific place within the mandala of the social network.

Since people relate in terms of roles and group expectations, they don't have to deal with the personal, emotional issues that come up between them. In terms of social cohesion and stability, that's a very functional system. Or it has been, in the premodern world.

VJD: So the self is subservient to the system you are a part of.

JW: That's right. In the East, the group always has more importance than the individual. And the exact opposite is true in the West. We value the individual and individual development, questioning authority, and finding our own path. We stress person-to-person intimacy. Of course, we in the West are certainly not any better at getting along with each other than people in the East. But the strong point of Western relationships is their potential for genuine intimacy.

VJD: Sure doesn't look like it. The news just bombards us with stories of us hurting one another.

JW: The major problem on the planet is that human beings have not learned how to get along with each other. To have more enlightened relationships, I believe we need to bring together the Western emphasis on individuation—the process of becoming a true person and learning to be yourself—with the Eastern emphasis on liberation, the journey of going beyond focusing on yourself altogether.

In learning how to open up to another and to ourselves, a relationship can be a spiritual practice in its own right. Historically, most religious traditions have looked at relationships—sexual relationships, at least—as a kind of distraction that took energy away from one's spiritual direction.

VJD: I think you describe what is needed on both sides of the world if we are to survive.

What is needed just seems impossible to ever happen.

JW: This is where the integration of psychology and spirituality could be helpful. The process of awakening—both on the individual and the collective levels—involves realizing the universal awake presence that is the very essence of our nature. This helps us to be fully present with one another.

Yet at the same time most of us suffer from tremendous interpersonal wounding. Human woundedness always has to do with relationships. The wound is always a relational one. It is about love. Unless we address and heal this wounding around love, it will be hard to be fully present with another person, no matter how much meditative realization we have had. This requires some psychological work on ourselves, seeing where we have shut down and why and bringing attention and awareness to those wounded places.

VJD: People act out their wounds, almost always blaming someone else.

JW: The wound is always about love. It's fairly universal, but worse in the West because our child-rearing patterns and the holding environment of the culture as a whole are very deficient. We walk around with a deep sense of not being loved, not feeling lovable or worthy, not able to love ourselves. And this shuts us down and cuts us off from our deeper, essential nature.

Since our feeling of not being loved as we are developed in our early relationships with others, we often carry an enormous amount of grievance against others as a result. It may have started with mother, in the family, but it becomes generalized to "other" as we grow up. We carry around a sense of "the bad other," the one who doesn't love me, who doesn't treat me right, who doesn't see or respect me. And this bad-other image can flare up at any moment and become projected on someone who crosses us. Road rage is one example.

VJD: And, on a societal level, in feuds and wars.

JW: Exactly. This explains one of the great enigmas of intimate relationships: how two people who claim to love each other more than anyone else in the whole world can, by exchanging just a few words, suddenly be at each other's throats. Why does the honeymoon always degenerate into this life-and-death struggle?

To understand this we need to recognize the generalized sense of grievance against the bad other we carry around inside, which is ready to take over at a moment's notice. Anyone can become the object of our grievance. Our thought process often goes like this: I knew it! I thought you were OK. I thought you were a good person. But you're just like all the others. But underneath that, what's really going on is: "I feel hurt. I don't know that I am lovable because I never felt truly loved. And you are making me feel this terrible hurt by the way you are treating me right now. You're just like all the rest, I'll show you that you can't treat me like this..."

This kind of projection also happens between nations. Because each individual carries this wound and this grievance, we act it out on the global level as well. Now that the cold war is over, we have to keep creating monsters out there! Psychologically we need to create an adversary as a way to project our hurt outside, and to try to get the upper hand, so we don't feel so vulnerable. So we project, retaliate and take the righteous position. In the Middle East and in the mutual *jihad*s of Christianity and Islam we see how the grievances held by both sides keep escalating.

VJD: So you are saying that the evolution of human life will either move toward that next step of learning to relate, to love each other and help each other resolve conflicts, or toward self-destruction?

JW: The religious traditions all stress the importance of loving your enemies, loving your neighbor as yourself, turning the other cheek, or having compassion for all sentient beings. These ideas are all essential and true! However, as prescriptions they don't work very well. You can't love your neighbor by believing that you should. Often these prescriptions create more guilt, making it even more difficult to love genuinely. You feel, I know I should love my neighbor. But the truth is that I don't love my neighbor, so that must mean I'm really bad. So trying to love your neighbor winds up making you hate yourself all the more.

VJD: So it seems the question is, can you go totally into that need for love and be there with it?

JW: We can start at any moment. Even though we've defended against it and buried it and denied it, our need for love drives everything we do. Whether I'm a CEO working eighty hours a week or a politician winning millions of votes or a best-selling author with ten books on the current list, the motivation is at bottom the same: I'm trying to win love, often in the form of approval, or respect, or admiration. That's our way of compensating for the sense of deficiency, the hole inside us, where we do not feel fully loved.

The drive for power also comes from the same need. To be powerful is a way of getting people to look up to you. Anyone can start at any moment to discover their real motivation. And as you start to do that, and go deeply within, you eventually find a place where you feel disconnected from love. Working with that can bring about real healing. It doesn't require going to meditate for five years on a mountaintop. Bringing awareness and compassion to the wounded place provides the kind of healing that will allow relationships to blossom on this planet.

When we can finally be present with the shut down place, fully and directly, then there is the possibility of healing where we meet ourselves in a new and deeper way. The focus on others as the source of our happiness or our sorrow distracts us from this deeper imperative of meeting ourselves. When we can feel and acknowledge the place where we are cut off and shut down, and unpack the pain and the old grievances stored up there, we become present in a place where we've been absent. This opens a doorway through which we gain access to our deeper nature— which is full of openness, love, and presence.

In this way, healing intersects with awakening. We find the true source of love. That source is trustworthy because it doesn't disappear. Standing on that ground, we can become whole human beings who can be present in relationships while also abiding in our own nature. And this can allow spiritual wisdom to flow more fully into this world.

It's only at this point in human history that we can explore the intersection of psychology and spirituality, human relatedness and liberation, becoming a person and going beyond the person altogether. Up until now the East has emphasized one direction, while the West has emphasized the other.

To be human is to be human and more-than-human at the same time. To live in duality and nonduality simultaneously. This is the koan for the evolution of humanity. This is the uncharted territory still waiting to be explored.

Norman Fischer
Being Everyday Zen

"Whenever you encounter the fact of what we conventionally call death in some-one, consider that an enormous privilege because it's a chance to see truth close up and deep. That person is your teacher."

"When you are truly aware of death, it's a serious and deep encounter with life."

POET AND FORMER ABBOT of the San Francisco Zen Center, Norman Fischer is founder and teacher of the Everyday Zen Foundation, a religious organization dedicated to sharing Zen teachings and practice widely. In addition to traditional Zen, he teaches Jewish meditation, and leads groups for business leaders, lawyers, and health care professionals working with the dying. He has authored a dozen books of poetry, and is the author most recently of *Taking Our Places: The Buddhist Path to Truly Growing Up* (HarperSanFrancisco, 2003). He lives in Muir Beach, California with his wife Kathie.

I drove to Mill Valley to interview Norman Fischer on one of those beautiful San Francisco winter days when the sun sparkles through the clear cold winds, glancing off the deep blue Bay currents. I was meeting him in his office/teaching space, where the Everyday Zen Foundation is based. Set at the end of a winding street, Norman's hideaway glass doors opened to welcome us as his hands reached out to greet us and offer tea after our travels. His deep brown eyes warmed as we shared news of mutual acquaintances. His smile and steady stream of words filled the small office where we spent the afternoon talking about his life, writing, and teaching till the sun had sunk over the hillside and the fog filled the landscape, making the journey back to Berkeley slow, slow going.

Victoria Jean Dimidjian: You fill so many different roles in your life. How do they come together?

Norman Fischer: Yes, I know: many parts, many streams. Probably too many! I have to figure out just who I'm supposed to be every day. Usually it's several people. Today was a day like that. I have many briefcases at home that I keep lined up in my study, and some days I pack several of them, each one filled with books and papers and tapes that have to do with different lives, different selves. I go out in the morning taking this one for that, and then this one for this, this one too, you know, for something else. It's actually rather fun, challenging.

VJD: In reading about your life, Norman, one place said you were born in Pittston, Pennsylvania, while another said Wilkes-Barre. Can you go back to the beginning for us?

NF: Pittston doesn't have a hospital, so I was born in Wilkes-Barre but grew up in Pittston.

My grandparents were immigrants from the Austro-Hungarian Empire. And for some reason a community of people from there and other parts of Eastern Europe settled in the Wilkes-Barre area, which is northeastern Pennsylvania, north of Philadelphia and south of New York. It was a small but very close-knit Jewish community. It is gone now. My parents were of the generation that followed the initial immigrants who established the community and founded the synagogue. They grew up together with the children of the immigrants in that place. That was the community I grew up in.

Pittston was a working-class town. Many Polish people. And lots of Irish, lots of Italians. Predominantly Catholic. I went to public schools, so my friends as I was growing up were a mixture of gentiles I went to school with and the Jewish community that was the social and religious center of our lives. Although there was respect and polite intercourse, by and large my parents never mixed with the non-Jews, and that was typical. All the communities were pretty separate.

VJD: Your description of your own Jewish community and yet the small town connections that existed, is that partially how you've been able to reach out across your life to so many different spiritual and cultural traditions?

NF: To tell you the truth, I can't account for it. My best guess is that it has to do with poetry. I entered religious practice not because of religion but because of poetry. Poetry was my avenue for exploration. I was always exploring, always trying to figure out what was going on, what was real, what life meant. And so it wasn't so much that I was faithful to this religion or that religion as much as I just want to find out what's actually going on. From an early age I saw that the usual explanations—or lack of explanations—did not hold up.

And when you work as a poet you have a tremendous sensitivity to language, of course. So I saw the different religious traditions as languages. If somebody asks me, "How could you possibly be a Buddhist and a Jew at the same time?" I say, "Well, there are people whose native language is French but they are fluent in German. So they have some real appreciation for German culture from the inside, but their language is French. If they spend enough time in Germany, then German is also their language, their reference point. And it changes how they speak and understand French. How can someone be bilingual? It seems to be possible. Even natural."

My religious beliefs are like that. Each religion has its own integrity, its own *gestalt*, and you can't mix them up, although, as with languages, there is always a certain amount of borrowing. But you can speak more than one.

So I think that sensitivity to language has given me a different approach to religion than the one I would've had if I was approaching religion primarily as a believer, a member of the faithful. I have never approached any religion as a member of the faithful.

As a kid I grew up a Jew. I was just given that. I accepted it without question. I was also a boy and not a girl; I accepted that, too. It never occurred to me to argue with it. But as soon as I started to think, I started to wonder about what the world was really about. It never occurred to me that Judaism had anything to do with that, just as being a man had nothing to do with that, in particular. These were just givens.

Poetry led me to Buddhism, which I practiced as a way of exploring reality more than as someone who converted to Buddhism, leaving off his previous religion. I never felt as if I converted to anything. I was just following my nose.

VJD: So as a kid you did have a family with definite religious traditions?

NF: Oh yes! I had a strong mentor, the rabbi of our congregation, Gabriel Maza, a most intelligent man. To give you an idea of his sensibility, let me tell you that his brother is Jackie Mason, the comedian. And he's just like Jackie! Restless intelligence, tremendous wit, great energy—all of that! And in our community he stood out. He was a young man, well read and curious. But the community was not an educated community, not an intellectual community at all. And he wanted somebody to talk to. I was 12 years old, and he said, "Here's somebody I can talk to." So we had a very intense study relationship, private lessons in Judaism which turned out to be private lessons in everything. We studied Aristotle, all kinds of avenues of Jewish thought, novels, you know, all of it. We did this, we did that, all kinds of things, all under the guise of studying for my Bar Mitzvah, which took about four years!

He was very influential in my life. He's still alive, and I still am close to him today. When I go to New York, I usually go to visit him. He's been on Long Island with a congregation there, for about forty years.

So I did have a strong sense of religious education, but that way. Very open. He was very faithful, observant Jew, but also very intelligent, very interested in the world, very wide in his scope, questioning. So that helped me to see life that way.

VJD: How did you come to poetry?

NF: That came when I learned to read. I started to read and that opened up right away. But there were no books in my house. Neither of my parents was educated, neither was a reader. And no library then in our little town! But somehow, some book fell into my hands. And I read it. It was a novel. It was a really dumb novel. *Freckles* by Gene Stratton Porter, a popular novelist of the Thirties who nobody even knows any more.

And the experience of imaginative literature blew my mind! I thought, this is amazing! Here you are walking around in a rather bleak, a rather small, world, and then all of a sudden you are in another world. That really impressed me. I savored that book. It took, it seemed, a hundred years to read. I think it was actually the first book I ever read. Freckles was a lumberjack or something like that.

VJD: You were seven or eight?

NF: Yeah, around that age. And that gave me the idea of writing. That's how I think you become a writer. You're really affected and moved by a piece of work, and then you think, I have to find a way to do this myself.

So I think all art comes out of imitation in that sense, an appreciation for art by others. And so from an early age I had that going on although it was rather vague, a feeling more than anything else.

VJD: What was it like when you left home?

NF: Yeah, I was very eager to go to Colgate College because there was no culture and no possibility to learn anything more in Pittston, at least that I could see. I knew that I was interested in philosophy, literature, sociology—I studied all of that stuff! And it was really a crapshoot what I would major in because I was studying all of it.

I'd been writing already, seriously writing. I actually wrote a whole volume of short stories and a novel before I got out of high school. And many poems, too. I had a professor at Colgate, Fred Busch, who was an up and coming young experimental writer. I think he's still alive though I haven't kept up with him. And I was in writing classes, hanging around with other literary types, writing for the literary magazine and the newspaper, so I was very much pointed toward being a writer.

When I left Colgate I went to the University of Iowa Writer's Workshop. The idea of just being a religious person or having a religious career didn't enter my mind. Far from it! It was probably the last thing I expected to do.

VJD: When did Buddhism come into your life?

NF: In Iowa I discovered books about Zen and I thought it was terrific. I thought, This is what I've been working toward! In Iowa I'd met someone who'd lived in San Francisco and practiced Zen there. I didn't know this was possible. I had been understanding Zen from a Western perspective, as a philosophy. You agree with it, you think about it, you make your own private efforts to figure out how to live by it. So when somebody said, "No, no, there's a practice. There's meditation, there are retreats, there's a person in San Francisco who teaches it." I said, "Fine, I'm going to do that."

I had no other plans. I was very impractical and not thinking about the future. So I said, "Okay, I'll do Zen like it says in the book and get enlightened and then see what happens next."

I had been intensely political through the late Sixties, and it really wore me out. I'd been arrested, beaten up by police, gone to interminable meetings, demonstrations, and so on. I was feeling as if pursuing desperate, romantic, radical politics was too tiring to be a life. So I thought going to California was breaking with all that and starting over again with Zen. Somehow I'll find a way to live in the mountains and be a hermit—that was my goal, although it was pretty vague.

I didn't know anybody, didn't have any contacts. Oh, wait, I had one! A friend of mine, Rabbi Alan Lew who is over in San Francisco now. We were very close friends at Iowa. This was many years before he even dreamed of becoming a rabbi. We'd both made the same decision to move to California. We didn't move together, and we didn't really make plans. But he moved, and then I did, and pretty soon we found each other and we spent a lot of time together. Somehow we never had a job so we could hang out for hours, days, at a time.

But other than him I didn't know anybody at all. One of the professors at Iowa had a friend who had a place where I could stay, so I initially stayed up in Eureka. And then I just sort of knocked around-—Northern California, north of the Bay area, and I did that for three or four years.

I'd gotten a terrific scholarship when I was an undergraduate. I don't know if it still exists. It was called the Danforth, and it was the greatest scholarship in the world. It gave you full tuition, full room and board, even a living stipend, just enough to get by on, just to study, and I always liked studying! I thought the university was silly in many ways, it made me restless, it was too perfect, too nice, but studying was great, you know? I could not pass up a deal like that. Anyway, the alternative was probably to get a job, in which I had no interest whatsoever. So at first I went to the University of Iowa, but then I had two more years on the Danforth. So after knocking around for three years—and in that time I had begun my Zen practice, and I was passionate about it, really wanted to continue— so I said, well, maybe I can go back and get another master's degree financed by the Danforth.

I went to a joint program with Berkeley and the Graduate Theological Union for a master's degree in religion with a concentration in Asian studies. But actually while I was in graduate school I also wasn't in graduate school because what I was really doing was intensely practicing in the Berkeley Zen Center. That was my community and that was my life.

I got hold of a couple of very understanding people who became my advisors. They understood that I really didn't want to hang around the university, what I really wanted to do was study Buddhism, so they allowed me to do a lot of independent study.

VJD: Is the Berkeley Zen Center still there?

NF: The Berkeley Center was started by Sojun Weitsman, who had been ordained by Suzuki Roshi, and Suzuki Roshi actually founded the Berkeley center as a kind of outpost of the San Francisco Center in about 1968 or 1969. When I went to the San Francisco Zen Center, I didn't like it. I found the Berkeley center much less objectionable. It was simpler, more informal.

Everyone in San Francisco was so serious, so pious. The place was fancy and the Buddha statues were too big. To this day a large Buddha statue seems excessive to me. Berkeley was much simpler. I much preferred that so I practiced there. And I liked Sojun a lot. I admired him. He was really my idea of a Zen master, not saying much, working in the garden, playing his recorder. I'd go to San Francisco Zen Center for lectures and long retreats, because I liked to listen to Baker-roshi, who gave interesting and challenging talks, but basically I lived and practiced in Berkeley for about five years.

VJD: And at the same time writing—

NF: Always writing! As I continued to think about and study Zen and get a better feel for my life, writing prose became less and less possible. I saw that writing was words, and I'd get hung up on words. Prose is explanatory, you're trying to make sense, but I found more and more I couldn't do that. The words were getting in the way. I was more interested in and driven to intuitive non-directive writing, feeling through the language, and that led me inevitably to poetry. There was no way I could write prose anymore! The experience I was having was too elusive. Doing Zen really made poetry possible, even necessary. So from about 1972 or '73 I was only writing poetry.

VJD: Your writing has sometimes been an interesting fusion of prose and poetry, particularly in *Whether or Not to Believe in Your Mind*.[1] Are you still experimenting?

NF: My writing has always been mostly about discovery, experimenting and discovering new forms and different ways of writing. It's anomalous that—practicing Buddhism and also teaching Jewish meditation and involved in Catholic dialogue—my writing is as wacky as it is. On the surface it doesn't sound religious at all. Often people present me as "a Zen poet" in readings, so audiences sometimes come with expectations about what that's going to be like—and then they can not figure it out because it's so unexpected. People who are expecting some sort of conventional poetry with an Asian Zen flavor are quite surprised. They don't know what to think. So…[laughing]…it's all kind of strange! I can't help it, you know…

VJD: But it's a wonderful structure you give to words. Unique in my experience. Trying to see the flow, the parts of experience…

NF: I'm just trying to figure out how to live. You know? I'm basically from then to now just trying to get through the day! [laughing] That's it! This all comes about as a consequence of that. It's not anything that I figured out or thought through. I'm not so good at thinking things through.

It's not a problem for me personally. Things have worked out okay. I eat every day, I have lots of friends, but I think as far as people being able to figure me out, you know, just where I belong, what pigeon hole I belong in, that's confusing for people.

VJD: Norman, you said earlier that the written word was your introduction to Buddhism, that through reading you saw a new reality, conceived a new way of living. And you've had many teachers in California and along the way. Now you've moved into the position of being that for other people...

NF: Yes, I suppose so! It's very odd. My view is that it makes no sense for someone to think they are a teacher or that they understand something definitive...to me this seems like an absurdity. A failure to appreciate how things actually are. Do you know what I mean? Seems like a ridiculous idea!

Of course one has to be willing to occupy the seat of teacher for the benefit of someone who needs that. I don't say, "Oh, I'm not your teacher." That would be going too far. I don't run away from students. That would be cruel.

I'm there for people, and we have these relationships in the Dharma. So that I understand. And I come forward with people. But I also understand that I'm just practicing side by side with people. I'm trying to understand more. I'm trying to grow in wisdom and to develop. I make mistakes, I'm confused. And I'm clear on that point. I enjoy my confusion. It's relaxing! Still, I'm always trying to understand, and I'm always starting from zero.

Every time I sit down to write a poem, I have no idea beforehand, I'm just trying to understand how to write. And in my study of Buddhist texts, I have no idea, I'm just trying to understand. That's my spirit.

VJD: If we can turn to your writing and teaching about death, Norman, I'd like to share a story of something that happened this week as I was hunting for some of your books in the Berkeley bookstores. A woman at Small Press Distributors not only found the couple of volumes I couldn't locate anywhere else, but she also told me a most moving story of how much you helped her and her husband when he was dying of cancer. Her name was Laura—

NF: Ah, Laura Moriarity. She's a dear friend, great person. And she herself is a great writer. Really, a wonderful writer. Many books.

Her husband's death was a terrible time. He was so young, maybe just forty if even that. But what a teacher he was for us! He was a poet. And he was also exploring his life through poetry just as I was, so when it came time for him to die…I remember the talks we would have. Times when we really got to the edge of what could be said, sitting for hours in his apartment in San Francisco, as the light changed in the window slowly. And he was so wise and so powerful in his understanding of what was happening! And so clear-sighted. Courageous. It was unbelievable. After those talks, we'd both be in a deeply peaceful state.

When he was in the hospital, it was harder because sometimes he was delirious or under the influence of the drugs. Then we just sat together quietly or talked a little bit. Those are experiences I cherish, enormously important experiences for me.

There have been so many experiences for me like that. Here I am, not just a nice clergy-person coming to visit, but having an ongoing relationship that was powerfully exploring this question of what is life and what is death. That would go on for some time. There have been a number of people that I have gone through that with, and each one I cherish and remember really, really well and think of them as my teachers. Still.

VJD: It seems death has always been a teacher for you. Has that always been a path? Do you know why?

NF: There's not a day that goes by without my many, many, many times reflecting upon death. Absolutely.

It started very early with me. You know, I just had this remarkable learning…I was in Mexico recently doing a retreat, and someone there said, "Would you please give a talk on your spiritual journey and how you came to be a master?" That really was exactly what she said! And I thought, Oh geez! What a ridiculous idea. To me the whole thing was crazy. "Spiritual journey." "Master." I have no idea what these terms might mean. I usually ignore requests like that. But then for some reason I decided to do this, to talk about it. And I learned several things that I never knew before.

Two big things I learned were about death. I grew up living with my grandparents as well as my parents. We were all in the same house. And from the time I was very young my grandfather was deathly ill. It was always like, "Sshhh" and he was very cranky, uncomfortable, unhappy, angry. It was scary for a little boy. And he died when I was about seven. I'd never thought about it before but I'm sure now that…you know, even though nobody talked about it…that feeling in the house that he was dying was there all the time.

That was one thing that I learned that I'd never thought about before. And the other thing was the effect that having been born right after the war had on me. My father was a returning soldier. I never thought about how much grief, denial, and confusion was under the surface that nobody ever talked about. It was not something that I was ever aware of, but I am sure that I took all this in. I felt all this very deeply without ever naming it until last December at the retreat when I decided to talk about "my spiritual journey."

So I think that's part of my connection to dying. Either that or maybe just karma. I was born with it, who knows? But from a very early age death was there for me. I thought about it a lot as a child. It was shocking to me. I was indignant. I remember thinking that the whole thing was a very bad idea, a faulty design! First of all, it was highly unjust. At least, well, a lot of people could die, okay, that's understood. But that no one would escape regardless of what you did about it—it didn't matter if you were good, tried hard, et cetera. You still couldn't escape. And I thought this is not right! [He laughs, shaking his head with this memory.] I don't agree with this, something is wrong, something is rotten in Denmark, and I have to investigate this. I think that's what fueled my religious feelings. That was always in the background.

That childish feeling became associated with a tremendous inwardness and darkness which I didn't necessarily identify. When I was little I remember this had to do with death, but as I got older it was not death per se but some inwardness which then got put on the back burner when I was an adolescent. Then there were things to do: girls, there's this, there's that, and I was a very normal adolescent running around doing sports and social stuff. I was very social then. But as a young child I was totally the opposite—withdrawn when I was little and my parents even thought there was something wrong with me. Who knows, maybe they were right!

Of course when you study Buddhism, the theme of death and impermanence does come up. Buddha harped on it all the time. It all begins and ends with impermanence. And from the standpoint of Dharma, thinking about death is very wholesome, very important, not morbid, as I had been led to believe. So I got credit for my madness! The recollection of death is seen in Buddhism as the recognition of the preciousness of life and the actual sense of what life really is. The path to appreciating life is the meditation on death.

In Japanese Buddhism, "birth" and "death" are just one word. There's not death and birth and life, it's life-and-death, or birth-and-death, just one hyphenated word. So there's no way to appreciate life without death. There's no way to be alive without death. Death is a moment by moment experience—we die each moment to the moment. This is not just a clever idea—it's really so. That's what time is. That's what being is.

Whenever you encounter the fact of what we conventionally call death in someone, consider that an enormous privilege because it's a chance to see truth close up and deep. That person is your teacher. I feel that way to this day. If I encounter a person who is dying and they ask me to talk with them, this person is my teacher. I'm here to learn from this person.

VJD: And you've been able to teach others about this?

NF: I wouldn't go so far as to say that I teach anything about death; I am just willing to sit still for it.

VJD: In *Jerusalem Midnight* you wrote about your mother's death, Norman. Was the poem there a way for you to come to a fuller acceptance?

NF: Well, I wrote that poem on a clear night at Tassajara, our monastery in the mountains, where it was deeply quiet and I could be truly reflective. And I was in touch with my mother. We were very close. She was there and there was a conversation going on. It wasn't like some big break through or some decisive moment, it was just one more moment in an ongoing series of conversations and encounters that I continue to have with my mother even though it's now a long time since she died. That was just one more moment that was intensely close…

VJD: Does it feel like death is more of a reality to you as you move into later life?

NF: Oh, absolutely, death is coming close, I feel that. I'm lucky that I'm pretty healthy but I have to think about my health. I have Crohn's disease and also spinal stenosis. Who knows what else I have! The body wears out a little bit more every day, no doubt.

Generally I feel great, all that hardly affects me. But I know my body is not what it was when I was younger, and I can feel it changing. I can feel death approaching. That's pretty indelible, I know it's there. And I often wonder about it. I very much can imagine and visualize—I often do!—death coming.

VJD: One of the things our culture now does as we have opened death as a reality is to ask how we prepare for it. Can you say more about that?

NF: Well, one thing is no one who's alive understands death. That's why a person who is close to it is our teacher. That's the most important thing we need to understand, and we can't really understand it unless we see that someone close to death understands it far better than we do. Even though they don't understand it either! So there's no way we can actually prepare. It's like jumping off a cliff, you know? There's no school for that!

But sometimes in meditation practice the mind becomes very, very quiet, and there is nothing arising, only silence, stillness, and letting go. And when that happens I think you have a very strong appreciation for something that is close to dying. And you realize that it's peaceful, a sense of completion and fullness...

Many times when life's challenges come up and you're resisting or you're dealing with it, and then you finally let go, it's also very much like death. There's a powerful traditional Buddhist practice which you do with a corpse. You recognize that the body that is in front of you is of the same nature as your own body. That body in front of you is now how your own body will soon be.

I always practice that when I am sitting with a person who has passed away. But I also do it many times a day, especially whenever something comes up to remind me. You know, like hearing that someone has died. I always have five or six people in my life who are facing death in one way or the other. So I make it a practice to think of them every day. It's not that they're dying and I'm not; it's that they are in a position that I am also in, and soon I will be more directly in as they are in right now.

And I feel that in my body, that feeling of dying, and I can visualize my own death and feel my own death—even though I recognize that it's not the same as that actually happening, of course!

I often try to put my mind in that place and my emotions in that place of my actual death. I can do it all the time. I was doing it today! Someone died, a public figure who was eighty-one years old. I heard about it today on public radio as I was driving over the bridge, and I thought, that person was eighty-one years old. That's not so many years from now. I may be eighty-one years old very soon. It really struck me, not unpleasantly but powerfully. In a way it made me feel more present, more alive, more serious about living in that moment, you know, and that's good. I appreciate that.

VJD: What you're describing is not just embracing death, just taking it in, but something more active, it seems. You're describing a way of living that acknowledges that death is already here.

NF: Right. Because that's what time is, right? Time tells us there is death every moment. And its wonderful to live that reality. What I appreciate is not pleasure per se or fun per se but really having a serious encounter with life. That's what I like. To me that's the deepest satisfaction, when you are truly aware of death, it's a serious and deep encounter with life.

VJD: So facing death isn't like a series of steps or doing certain things?

NF: No, no, it's not like that! It's a way of living, a meditation practice, the most fundamental and most profound of all meditation practices. I think that death is the most powerful of all the concentrations, our greatest teaching.

VJD: You've written about your own parents' aging process and their pain. I often see despair in old people that I know in Florida. How do you see helping with that?

NF: Ahh, who knows if we really ever help anybody! But, you see, I think that we each have two lives: the life you know about, the life of the things you did and the relationships you had, this and that, all that, and then another life, one that everybody has, but few of us really know about. In this life we are simply human beings who are born and who die. And that is profound. Everybody lives that life. On that level everybody is a courageous and dignified person because they've suffered to be born, they've suffered to live through their lives, and they accepted death and they gave their lives up. There is something really noble about that.

A person who doesn't see that second life can easily review their own life story and think that's the whole story. They can be happy about that or proud of it or ashamed of it or whatever they feel, but actually either way it doesn't make any difference, you know! Because the real life is the second life. And in that life, no matter what your life has been, there's a dignity.

Someone who has the privilege to be with an elderly or dying person— if they understand that about their own life and about life in general— then they have the eyes to see that in another person. They will always see a noble and beautiful person regardless of how the person *kvetche*s or complains or is crabby. They will have the eyes to see that here is a human being who's enduring the indignity and pain of old age, in a bad mental or emotional state maybe, but they're enduring it. They exist in the midst of it. And they are suffering it somehow. There's nobility in that. Always, always.

From a Buddhist point of view, one way to look at every human being is to say in terms of one life: they suffer, they die, they don't understand and they're reborn in miserable states. And on and on! But from another point of view—a bigger Buddhist view or just a bigger view, period—everybody who dies enters nirvana. Death-absence-cessation is nirvana. It's not that you explain that to somebody who is dying. Explaining has nothing to do with it. It's just that you relate to them on that basis. There can be some comfort in just being treated in that way, with that degree of respect.

Then there's the whole question of spiritual practices or counseling that can be given. But that's all actually rather trivial to this central issue. It all has to come from this, this place. [He gestures with wide arms.] If a person is open to it, there are many ways, you can practice with them.

I feel that the meditation practice that we do is simply meditation on coming to feel the feeling of being alive. That's the second level that I've been talking about, just feeling that. You sit down, you breathe, you feel the body, you feel the breath, you feel being alive, you feel being a human being. You actually feel what that feels like! Usually we're too busy for that, such a simple thing. Because we have problems, we have things on our list to do, we don't have time to recognize life.

This meditation is a simple practice a person can do lying in bed, even in dimmed consciousness, regardless what they believe or don't believe. This can be explained in terms of any religion. This takes a little bit of imagination and a little bit of courage and little love but not so much, you know, just this much [Norman holds his hands just apart], that's all we need to apply this practice to any tradition.

VJD: That makes so much sense to me. I wonder how you move from this world of working with the individual to your social concerns. You seem to remain connected to the world of politics and social realities. Do you feel yourself pulling away from that involvement as you turn more to working with the dying and the teaching of Buddhism?

NF: I'm still socially concerned, but I have to say I feel naïve, uninformed. I try but I don't read a newspaper every single day. I listen to the radio, try to know what's going on, but I don't try to speak about social issues from the standpoint of practice because I don't feel well enough informed. It's partly a practical matter. My days are extremely full. I have a lot of bases to cover. And then there is my unfortunate poetry habit to take care of. So it would be impossible for me to read much about what goes on. And anyway I am very impatient with so much of the detail of this stuff— there is so much repetition and so much useless stuff. The news is probably ninety percent nonsense. Cluttering of the mind with no purpose.

My heart is socially active, and I do lend myself to socially active causes and concerns but I'm just not as informed as a lot of other people are. Still, I do speak out. I wrote several essays about September 11 that were published and given as talks, and now I have been writing and speaking about the war in Iraq—another horrifying mistake.

VJD: Between your Buddhist teachings, your social concerns, and all your work, where does writing fit in? I was amazed that you wrote *Success*, creating a poem of 28 lines each day of the year.[2] Do you set up a regular time for writing as you do for meditation?

NF: I write most days, but no, not in the same way that I sit in meditation, first thing in the morning, or on a schedule. I write when I need to, usually in the morning before I think about anything else. If I haven't written in a couple days, I feel it, I am out of sorts, and I know it's time to write something. And then I make it a priority. And usually several things go to hell as a result. But I am used to that. I have developed tolerance for chaos. Every day I find far more that is necessary for me to be doing than can be done. So every day I think, where will I fail, fall short today? And then I say, well, I fell short in poetry yesterday and the day before, so today it is most important even though I have other pressing things. So I write. Everything else disappears.

VJD: Because that's part of who you are—

NF: It just seems to be a necessity. But it's very complicated being a person, isn't it? Just the maintenance alone is a huge job! You've got to take your vitamins, keep your body functioning, floss your teeth, and every one of those thirty-two teeth has to be brushed several times a day [he laughs] and then you've got to do your laundry—it's really a big job! And then there's poetry, and if you want to keep your mind active, you have to read something, and then you have your spiritual life, and maybe you have people in your life, people you have relationships with, and you have to be sure they're okay. And if they have trouble you have to be by their side. And then if you have children or family, you have to be a person there, too. I don't know how anybody does it. It's amazing, you know! Really, it's a miracle, actually a miracle how we do all these things!

And in any given area of my life, I'm always miserably failing. Definitely! I'm serious now, you know, and I'm trying to feel a little bit less a failure. Life is so demanding, and one just can't do justice to it. So you try your best in a sinking ship to do what you can till the ship goes down. And then you're relieved of all these troubles. And you can be happy, finally— [he gives a great belly laugh here]—at the bottom of the ocean!

Every day I have to make many adjustments. I have the blessing and the curse of no fixed schedule. So every day I have to figure out what I'm doing, which brief cases I have to pack up and carry, and some times during the day things change and I have to try to go with that. For many years when I was an administrator for the San Francisco Zen Center, life was more structured. Now with Everyday Zen there's almost no structure, no schedule. Every day I figure it out. And my teaching, studying, lecturing is important work but it's a different mind than poetry. And different than planning and administration. I still have to do a certain amount of that. And my calendar is the bane of my existence. I can't delegate that. I work real hard at being less wild, less complaining.

But we're all CEO's of the body, CEO's of the mind. And our worlds have to be organized, we have to do that. Every day, every moment, being here.

VJD: And your way of doing it is a guide for us through the fun as well as the sound and fury of life. A last word or two to conclude?

NF: Well after all this talk about poetry I should conclude with today's poem. This is just scribbled out this morning so it might not be a very good poem, maybe raw, but it is fitting for this discussion anyhow.

1 Norman Flischer, *Whether or Not to Believe in Your Mind* (Great Barrington, MA: The Figures Press, 1987).

2 Norman Fischer, *Success* (Philadelphia, PA: Singing Horse Press, 2000).

NORMAN'S POEM:

The tabernacle above in the clouds
Is here staked into the packed earth
Its cloth walls streaming
In the hot wind same tabernacle
Also as one of stone spattered with blood
Childhood's wall that is servant of the tyrant truth—
    The things that can't be said out loud

What's that? Who's talking? Who listens?

But without passion
In that sacred space, a field of rock, almost anything
Will (will not) occur
To you and you walk
Like a blind man
Out onto the plain
Of pain, suspended
    From above

Not now, not later, but just
Next, in the next
Expectant moment of slashing
Intentions do you think
You know whereof you speak, that you
Hear the boatswain's song
Lapping
    Of the waves?

Lower that one, shrink this one
Bust open the stones—

In the side street, in the crowded street
Among the various donkeys, not sea creatures
    The one in the shadow is aware

Resources for Continuing the Conversation

This section contains materials from each interviewee and some personal favorites; including ten audiovisual resources, thirty outstanding books and seven activities you may want to initiate. Best wishes for your lifelong journey!

AUDIOVISUAL RESOURCES

"*Conscious Aging: On the Nature of Change and Facing Death*"—a two-part audio tape series. Ram Dass recorded this live in 1992 with stories from his own life, his work with the dying since 1966 and the lessons of aging he now knows from living—available from Sounds True at 800-333-9185 or www.soundstrue.com, Boulder, CO: Sounds True Recordings, 1992.

"*Why Suffering?*" where Ram Dass explores one of the most baffling spiritual questions and shares his metaphysical response—from RDTapes at 800-248-1008 or www.RamDassTapes.org

"*Fierce Grace*" is a documentary about Ram Dass's last few years during which "stroke yoga" has been the blessed practice of his daily life. It is available on videotape or DVD commercially or from the Tape Library or at many university and community libraries. New York: Zeitgeist Video 2003, 2001.

"*Becoming a compassionate Companion: Teaching, Stories and Practical Wisdom for those Accompanying Someone who is Dying*" is an audio series by Frank Ostaseski which was produced and can be obtained through the Zen Hospice Project at 273 Page Street in San Francisco, CA 94102 (415-863-2910), www.zenhospice.org

"Graceful Passages: A Companion for Living and Dying" is a set containing a small, book and two compact discs which contains words and music for those living the end-of-life journey. It can be obtained through www.gracefulpassages.com.

My own favorite is the CD *"Drops of Emptiness"* which contains songs, chants and poetry from Thich Nhat Hanh, Sister Chân Không and the monks and nuns at Plum Village. It is available from Sounds True at 800-333-9185 or www.soundstrue.com, Boulder, CO, 1997.

"The Heart of Spiritual Practice," Hay House Audio. Jack Kornfield and Michael Toms. Carlsbad, CA, 1997.

Bill Moyers' four-part PBS series, *"On Our Own Terms"* explores issues of aging, end-of-life care, choices in death and family/social responsibility. Princeton, NJ: Films for the Humanities and Sciences, 2000. www.pbs.org/onourownterms

"Walk Me to the Water: Three People in their Time of Dying" is a video by John Seakwood that movingly depicts the needs of three individuals at the end-of-life and their families. Available by phone: 518-794-8081. New Lebanon, NY, 1981.

INTERNET RESOURCES

Webster's Death, Dying & Grief Guide:
http://www.katsden.com/death /index/html
This site carries a large range of topics as well as numerous helpful links.

Growth House: http://www.growthhouse.org
An award-winning Website that offers resources, links, chat room, and online bookstore.

Compassion in Dying is an Oregon-based Internet site offering information and support in end-of-life choices.
http://www.CompassionInDying.org or call 503-221-9556.

Center to Improve the Care of the Dying in Washington, D.C. offers research, education and advocacy at 202-467-2222 or http://www.gwu.edu/~cicd.

George Washington Institute for Spirituality and Health in Washington, D.C. works in clinical, educational, policy, and advocacy fields and can be reached at 202-496-64009 or http://www.gwish.org.

BOOK RESOURCES

John Archer. *The Nature of Grief: The Evolution and Psychology of Reactions to Loss.* (London and New York: Routledge Press, 1999). Using three approaches—evolutionary, ethological, and psychological—Archer takes the reader on an historical survey in understanding loss and grief.

Ernest Becker. *The Denial of Death.* (New York: Free Press, 1973). This seminal work opened scholarly and public dialogue on death and problems existing in a death-denying culture.

Ira Brock, M.D. *Dying Well: Peace and Possibilities at the End of Life.* (New York, Riverhead Books, 1998). One of the best Western medical attempts at addressing the end-of-life process today.

Sister Chân Không's life-story in *Learning True Love: How I Learned and Practiced Social Change in Vietnam* (Berkeley, CA: Parallax Press, 1993) expands many of themes in this interview and describes the separate stages in her work in engaged Buddhism. Author listed: Cao Ngoc Phuong.

Ram Dass. *Be Here Now, Remember* (New York: Hanuman Foundation, Distributed by Crown Publishing, 1971). Richard Alpert's journey East resulting in his transformation into Ram Dass has continued to inspire readers since its publication and to represent the dynamic integration of Eastern wisdom into Western culture.

Ram Dass. *Still Here: Embracing Aging, Changing and Dying.* (New York: Riverhead Books, 2000). Ram Dass had completed much of this book before his stroke, but the personal encounter with facing his own death and daily dependence on others has deepened his practice and his understanding of reality.

Michael Eigen. *Damaged Bonds* (London, New York: Karnac Books, 2001) and *Ecstasy* (Middleton, CT: Wesleyan University Press, 2001). These recent books illustrate Eigen's skill in exploring human issues and lives with his patients and within his own psyche.

Michael Eigen. *The Psychoanalytic Mystic* (London, New York: Free Association Books, 1998). This work is unique in its dynamic interweaving of psychoanalytic tradition, spiritual wisdom and humanistic individualism. I also recommend exploring the articles in Anthony Molino's *The Couch and the Tree: Dialogues in Psychoanalysis and Buddhism.* (New York: North Point Press, 1998) which contains an intriguing interview with Dr. Eigen as well as interviews with others in the forefront of East-West psychology today.

Mark Epstein. *Thoughts without a Thinker: Psychotherapy from a Buddhist Perspective.* (New York: Basic Books, 1995). This acclaimed first work by a now well-known Western psychologist integrates Buddhism into clinical theory and practice.

Norman Fischer. *Jerusalem Moonlight: An American Zen teacher walks the path of his ancestors.* (San Francisco: Clear Glass Press, 1995). This remarkable extended essay weaves Norman's exploration of his heritage with his work as a Buddhist leader, his roles as family member, creative artist, and world citizen and his finding meaning in each day's living experience.

Norman Fischer. *Taking Our Places: The Buddhist Path to Truly Growing Up.* (Harper San Francisco, 2003.) Based on his earlier work with Bay Area adolescents, Fischer here explores Buddhist themes as connecting to adolescence, parenting, education and social change.

Stanislav Grof and Joan Halifax. *The Human Encounter with Death.* (New York: E.P. Dutton, 1977). A groundbreaking work exploring the boundaries of life and death through psychological and pharmaceutical journeying.

Jerome Groopman. *The Anatomy of Hope: How People Prevail in the Face of Illness.* (New York: Random House, 2004). This just-published study of individuals and families facing end-of-life dilemmas is deeply moving and realistic, written by a Harvard medical school professor who opens his own life struggles as he learns from others.

Thich Nhat Hanh's recent book *No Death, No Fear: Comforting Wisdom for Life*. (New York: Riverhead Books, 2002) contains teachings most relevant to this interview and exploring the meaning of the end of our individual lives. Two other excellent books by Thich Nhat Hanh which further expand this exploration are *Creating True Peace: Ending Violence in Yourself, Your family, Your Community and the World* (New York: Free Press, 2003) and *The Blooming of a Lotus: Guided Meditation for Achieving the Miracle of Mindfulness* (Boston, MA: Beacon Press, 1993).

Elisabeth Kubler-Ross. *Questions and Answers on Death and Dying*. (New York: Macmillan, 1974) and *Death: The Final Stage of Growth* (Englewood Cliffs, NJ: Prentice-Hall, 1975). Kubler-Ross opened the door to discussion of death and learning from the dying, and these works of hers are classics.

Elisabeth Kubler-Ross and David Kessler. *Life Lessons: Two Experts on Death and Dying Teach us about the Mysteries of Life and Living*. (New York: Scribner, 2000). Dr. Kubler-Ross continues to teach even as she struggles with disability and pain at the end of her own life journey.

Stephen Levine. *Who Dies?: An Investigation of Conscious Living and Conscious Dying*. (Garden City, NY: Anchor Press/Doubleday, 1982). This was the book which led Rodney Smith—among many others committed to lives of service—to hospice work and still stands as one of most important contributions to the field. Levine's work continues to be central to understanding death and dying. His latest book *Turning Toward the Mystery: A Seeker's Journey* (Harper San Francisco, 2002) is the deeply moving story of his own life and learning.

Joanne Lynn, Joan Harrold, and the Center to Improve Care of the Dying. *Handbook for Mortals: Guidance for People Facing Serious Illness*. (New York and Oxford: Oxford University Press, 1999). This is a sensitive yet straightforward manual to be used by those facing death and those who love and care for them.

Janice Winchester Nadeau. *Families Making Sense of Death.* (Thousand Oaks, CA: Sage Publications, 1998). Written with the care giver or health care provider in mind, this work explores helping families and patients during the illness and dying process.

Rinpoche, Sogyal. *The Tibetan Book of Living and Dying.* (Harper San Francisco, 1992). This commentary on the ancient classic, *Tibetan Book of the Dead,* from the East has been the central focus of Westerners developing practices of conscious dying for the past decades and continues to be focal in understanding this step in the living/transforming process. Other authors listed: Patrick Gaffney and Andrew Harvey.

Kathleen Singh. *The Grace in Dying: How We Are Transformed Spiritually as We Die* (Harper San Francisco, 1998). This moving work describes the opening, growing and transforming possibilities offered to us as we learn to live with dying.

Rodney Smith. *Lessons from the Dying* (Boston: Wisdom Publications, 1998) provides case studies and discussion of the dying and their caregivers in hospice settings using the themes in this conversation.

Suzuki, D.T. *Mysticism: Christian and Buddhist.* (New York: Routledge, 2002). First published by Harper in 1957, this early work and all others by Suzuki are regularly cited by interviewees in this book and others who have "journeyed East" as the first transforming written words opening the passage for many Westerners.

Suzuki, D.T., Erich Fromm, and Richard DeMartino. *Psychoanalysis and Buddhism.* (New York: Harper Collins, 1986). First published in 1960, this was the first effort at integrating Eastern/Western psychological paradigms and practices.

Froma Walsh and Monica McGoldrick. *Living Beyond Loss: Death in the Family.* (New York and London: W.W. Norton, 1991). This collection of thoughtful, scholarly and deeply personal essays addresses loss of a family member from the family systems theoretical perspective with much sensitivity

John Welwood (Editor). *Awakening the Heart: East/West Approaches to Psychotherapy and the Healing Relationship.* (Boston: Shambhala Publications, 1983). In this early work John presents an East/West framework for working with different states of mind and emotion.

John Welwood. *Journey of the Heart: The Path of Conscious Love* (New York: Harper Collins, 1990). A broad overview and exploration of relationship as a path of personal and spiritual development; some of the areas covered include: passion, surrender, commitment, wildness, beginner's mind, aloneness, marriage, sex, male/female issues, sacredness, the razor's edge, breaking open the heart, the nature of path, and the relevance of meditation to relationship. This book was the first book to thoroughly lay out the path of conscious relationship.

John Welwood. *Love and Awakening: Discovering the Sacred Path of Intimate Relationships.* (New York: Harper Collins, 1996). This sequel to *Journey of the Heart* looks at relationship as a spiritual path, exploring its challenges as opportunities to recover lost dimensions of our being.

John Welwood. *Toward a Psychology of Awakening: Buddhism, Psychotherapy, and the Path of Personal and Spiritual Transformation.* (Boston: Shambhala, Publications 2000). A groundbreaking book, bringing together John's thirty years of work on the intersection of Eastern and Western psychology.

SUGGESTED ACTIVITIES

✦ Call and schedule an introductory visit to your local hospice; begin to think about if and when you might use this service for yourself or a family member.

✦ All hospice programs rely on trained volunteers for caretaking but also for help in maintaining the program and community activities, fundraising, outreach—explore options for involvement and volunteering.

✦ Take classes at your local college or university on human development and issues in aging/dying —many states offer these to older citizens for free or at a reduced charge.

✦ Spend quiet time alone in reading, thinking, and defining what "a good death" is for you now.

✦ Talk with your family and close friends about your ideas of "a good death" and what they may need to do to help you with this part of the life journey.

✦ Make concrete and carefully-written documents needed for your dying and death: will, durable power of attorney, living will, last directives, and last letters/videos/good-byes for all those you cherish in your heart.

✦ Schedule time with closest friends to view videos and films that address the last stage of life, talking and sharing the understandings and feelings you each gain from others' experiences.

✦ Engage in practices—meditation, prayer, study, working with others— to deepen your experience living and dying as one, being increasingly open to every moment and learning from each as you step footstep-by-footstep on your life-journey.